Organization Paremiology
A New Approach to Organizational performance Improvement

Adonis & Abbey Publishers Ltd
St James House
13 Kensington Square,
London, W8 5HD
United Kingdom

Website: http://www.adonis-abbey.com
E-mail Address: editor@adonis-abbey.com

Nigeria:
Suites C4 & C5 J-Plus Plaza
Asokoro, Abuja, Nigeria
Tel: +234 (0) 7058078841/08052035034

British Library Cataloguing-in-Publication Data
A catalogue record for this book is available from the British Library

ISBN: 978-1-909112-63-6(dust Jacket)
ISBN: 978-1-909112-59-9(paperback)

Organization Paremiology

A New Approach to Organizational performance Improvement

Chiku Malunga

ADONIS & ABBEY
PUBLISHERS LTD

Synopsis

Organization Paremiology: A New Approach to Organizational Improvement announces the future of organizational improvement efforts in Africa and the world by introducing a new field of study and practice called Organization Paremiology. It discusses what Organization Paremiology is, what it is constituted of, its key principles and its practice. It also discusses why Organization Paremiology is needed to form a new narrative in development and business talk in Africa and in the World. This book introduces and establishes an authentic and definitive Afrocentric contribution to organizational performance improvement at the global level.

Table of content

INTRODUCTION

Organization Paremiology is a new field of organizational performance improvement. This is the first book that is consciously aimed at explaining what Organization Paremiology is, why it is needed, why it is needed now and how it is carried out in practice.

Organization Paremiology means using the wisdom in (African) proverbs and folktales as a tool to improve the performance of organizations. The work of Organization Paremeiology is concerned with improving performance. We have done this work for the past 20 years. There have been more than 10 books published on various interventions of Organization Paremiology. These include works on Leadership Development, Strategy, Self-Development and the role of Spirituality in Organization Development.

The introduction of this new field of Organization Paremiology has raised a lot of interest and questions, hence this volume. This current volume therefore aims at bringing together the key principles and practices upon which Organization Paremiology will be built. Being the first book on the subject, it is understood that it will be more of an introductory and 'light' piece in nature. It is our hope that building on the current growing interest in the field of Organization Paremiology, many people will be interested in the book and, more importantly, that many academics and practitioners will build on it to create a more well-articulated and stronger field of Organization Paremiology.

This volume has also linked poverty in Africa with Organization Paremiology by asking and answering the question; Why is Africa poor? One reason is that for a long time as Africans, we have been walking on borrowed clutches of development and business models. We were convinced that we were lame when we were not. It is time to throw away the borrowed clutches and begin to walk on our healthy feet.

Organization Paremiology represents this consciousness which, for a long time, we called African renaissance.

Unlike the African renaissance discourse which is now quieter than it was a few years ago, the Organization Paremiology discourse will grow. The organization Paremiology discourse will grow because it is well articulated. For example, this book clearly and simply presents what Organization Paremiology is, why we need it, and why now? Then, it proceeds to present the four key tools of Organization Paremiology and summarizes the key principles upon which Organization Paremiology is based.

In the second and last part of the book, the practice of Organization Paremiology is presented by giving a general process of the practice, a few practical examples of Organization Paremiology at the organizational, community and national levels. The book discusses the development and role of the Organization Paremiologist before concluding with a reflection on the future of an organization based on Organization Paremiology.

Paremiology has been the essence of African life. In Africa, we believe that insight, more than foresight or even hindsight, is what we need the most in this ever increasingly complex and fast moving world. Insight is the essence of Paremiology. Insight is the essence of Organization Paremiology.

Despite Paremiology being the essence of African life, it is not surprising that Organization Paremiology is literally non-existent today. This is because we live in a world where the knowledge we are working with is largely colonial in nature. Up to now there is no African model that has been taken at global magnitude to guide development and business thought and practice. One of the negative effects of colonialism is that it destroyed the economic, social and cultural foundations of the local people. In Africa, the key capital that colonialism destroyed was the indigenous wisdom of the people. The colonists did this by telling the people that their local wisdom was irrelevant and retrogressive – so they needed to drop it and replace it with Western knowledge.

This colonial brain washing is still strong even up to now. It can be seen in the school systems, in the work systems, in worship, in music and even in language. English and French and to some extent Portuguese are languages for people with money in Africa. They are languages for the educated. One of the greatest needs of Africa today is post-colonial knowledge and practice. Organization Paremiology is one such need. Organization Paremiology is needed for Africa so that she is using her wisdom for her own benefit. It is also needed for the whole world.

The onslaught of globalization is getting stronger and stronger. The key question this raises is: what is going to happen in the future? Will the whole world become Westernized? Will we be strong enough to resist and maintain our African identity, which we have already mostly lost? These are very difficult questions to answer. But life is dynamic. Change is the only constant in life today. The challenge we have is one of choice. There are good African things and bad African things. There are good Western things and bad Western things. We need to choose the good African and good Western things and jettison the bad ones. This is the essence of this book. Organization Paremiology does not mean going back to a dead past. It means creating the future we want using on our rich unique heritage. From the four tools of Organization Paremiology presented in this book, it can be clearly seen that a new narrative in Africa will be based, among other things, on spirituality, natural science, culture and philosophy.

It is time that Universities in Africa were made in the image of Africa. It is time that practitioners demonstrate global level distinction that is rooted in local realities. In the words of Dr. Carlos Lopes, "Africa is ready for a big revolution, but we need a new narrative. This new narrative is in who we have always been – Organization Paremiology."

Organization Paremiology goes beyond adding a proverb or a folktale or two to an old familiar story or discourse. It is a way to recreate our world and reality. It is a rejection of the world as it has been given to us and a refashioning into the way we want it to be, based on our heritage. Organization Paremiology is based on the belief and conviction that the mind is not a vessel to be filled but a fire to be kindled (Belaynah, 2013). Organization Paremiology teaches us that we must trust ourselves more than we trust others.

Organization Paremiology

Organization Paremiology is a field aimed at improving organizational performance and impact. Paremiology means the study of proverbs. Organization Paremiology is the use of the indigenous wisdom in the proverbs to improve performance in organizations. Organization Paremiology also includes the use of the wisdom in folktales for communicating organizational issues. So, Paremiology is closely related to parables. A parable is an earthly story with a spiritual meaning. If we understand this principle, then we understand Organization Paremiology – a light story with deep meaning and with deep organizational implications. The four key tools of Organization Paremiology are: parables, metaphors, aspects of (African Culture), and (African) Proverbs and Folktales.

Organization Paremiology is built on a relatively better known field of Organization Development. Organization Paremiology represents the first idea in the world to consciously combine African indigenous wisdom contained in proverbs and folktales with the theory of organisation development.

Why Organization Paremiology?

By using African proverbs, Organization Paremiology simplifies, deepens and clarifies the otherwise relatively complex subject of Organization Development or Organization Capacity Development. Proverbs are an integral part of African culture. They are simple statements with deep meaning, serving as guidelines for individual, family, community and village behaviour, as built upon repeated real life experiences and observation over time. For example, a proverb like "if the sun says it is more powerful than the moon then let it come and shine at night" speaks about the importance of respecting roles and responsibilities in organizations. "The river that forgets its source will soon dry up" talks about the importance of values in an organization. One good proverb can explain adequately what a classic Organization Development Book requires a chapter to do. In other words, Organization Paremiology builds a complex issue into one sentence or story that is rich in its meaning.

Organization Paremiology deals with issues of visioning, learning, problem solving and ensuring impact among many other things in helping the organization to improve its performance. For example, Organization Paremiology work has been done on financial and organizational sustainability, leadership development, strategic thinking and planning, team building, self-development and the role of spirituality in organization development.

Conclusion

Organization Paremiology: Principles and Practice announces the future of organizational improvement efforts in Africa and the world by introducing a new field of study and practice called Organization Paremiology. It discusses what Organization Paremiology is, what it is constituted of, its key principles and its practice. It also discusses why Organization Paremiology is needed to form a new narrative in development and business talk in Africa and in the World. This book introduces and establishes an authentic and definitive Afrocentric contribution at the global level

CHAPTER ONE

Why Organizational Paremiolgy?

Introduction

Organization Paremiology fills a big need in Organizational Improvement studies and practice in Africa and the world today (Malunga, 2010). In the face of increasing organizational challenges, the level of knowledge and practice to deal with them remain significantly low. All the models accepted and employed so far have been developed in the West. These models have a worldview that may not always be congruent with the local realities in Africa. The fact that Organization Paremiology originates from and is rooted in Africa ensures more effectiveness in the Organizational Improvement efforts of practitioners on the continent, especially in ensuring more legitimacy, relevance and sustainability of results.

Organizational consciousness

Organization Paremiology is based on the African worldview of Ubuntu – the African concept and philosophy of community and the essence of being human. The Ubuntu cosmos is holistic. It encompasses the material and the spiritual. The spiritual reality is accepted without question. It is believed the human being is a spiritual being. However, this consciousness is absent from the modern worldview we mostly work with. As a result, most people are unconscious of this fact of their spirituality.

In Ubuntu thinking, a person becomes 'spiritually conscious' or 'spiritually alive' the day he or she discovers why they were put on earth. Spirituality relates closely to purpose. For some, this occurs spontaneously. For some, it is a gradual evolution which unfolds almost unconsciously. For others, it does not happen at all throughout all their life. They sleep walk their way through life. The same is true for organizations.

Human beings are trinity beings. They comprise the body, the mind (soul or the self) and the spirit. The current worldview causes human beings to be more conscious of their outer elements than their inner elements. For example, all human beings are aware that they have a body. Most are aware that they have a mind, and very few are aware that they have a spirit. In fact, not many people can locate where their spirit is.

The same is true with organizations. Organization Paremiology shows that organizations have bodies, minds and spirits. The body of the organization includes its material and financial resources. The organization's mind consists of its skills and competences; policies, systems and procedures; its structure: roles and responsibilities and its strategy. The spirit of the organization comprises its culture, values and norms; leadership; and vision and mission.

Understanding organizational spirituality

Organizational spirituality is a complex and simple concept to explain. There are so many lenses one can use to conceptualize the spiritual organization. These include:

- The Spirit – the ultimate source of all energy inspiration to the organization
- Organizational spirit - the organizational leadership, culture, values, norms, vision and mission
- Mind – Strategy, structure, roles and responsibilities or job description; policies, systems and procedures; skills and competencies
- Body - financial and material resources

A key point to make about organizational spirituality is the systemic nature of the idea. Everything is connected to everything. The source of spirituality is the Spirit, and then it flows outwards to all parts of the organization. It is not possible, for example, to have a good spiritual organization when the organization has a 'sick body'. It is not possible also to have an effective organization by working only on the 'spirit of the organization'. It is important to remember that when the consciousness of the role of the Spirit is well applied, this has an enhancing effect on all the parts of the organization holistically.

Organization Paremiology – The cultivation of effective organizations

Organization Paremiology aims at creating more effective organizations based on the understanding of Ubuntu, (Malunga, 2009). A number of characteristics identify an effective organization. Some of these are:

Self-consciousness

The greatest of all faults is to be conscious of none

Lack of organizational consciousness is a major cause of organizational failure. There is a lot of knowledge on organizational management, but not as much knowledge on organizational consciousness – what organizations are, how they grow and develop over time, what stages they pass through, what the issues related to these stages are and, most importantly, the consciousness around these processes.

As a result of this lack of knowledge and information, many organizations do not know what stage of development they are in, what challenges to anticipate and how to prepare for them. A key distinguishing feature of effective organizations is their organizational consciousness. Organization Paremiology emphasizes raising organizational consciousness

A dead rooster does not crow

Being self-conscious also means developing capacity for self-critique. A president of an African country asked his counterpart from another country why he had so many demonstrations and strikes in his country. The other president responded by saying that it was because he was leading people who were alive. He said dead people do not talk. He said his people were demonstrating because they were alive.

If we have no dissent or opposing views in our organization, chances are high that we are leading people who are not alive. The more we discourage dissent, the more we suffocate organizational life. Dissent is a sign of self-consciousness.

> Becoming conscious is becoming aware of something and then acting responsibly in light of the new awareness. It is not synonymous with awareness alone, as some dictionaries state.

> Responsible action is another element of human consciousness. Responsible action does not mean acting compulsively or reactively. It means choosing consciously, resulting in the least number of unintended consequences. The conscious organization is a group of people who are constantly examining their individual and collective consciousness.

Clear sightedness

What the elders see while sitting, young ones standing on their toes wont see

Organization Paremiology emphasises the role of effective leadership. In an effective organization, leadership means articulating the vision of the organization. Vision means sight. It means seeing. The vision of the organization is the intended destination of the organization. Vision therefore means communicating where the organization is going. An effective organization therefore has the clearest sight about where the organization is going. A distinguishing feature of an effective organization is its clear and deep sense of purpose.

A positive outlook on change

All great truths begin as blasphemies

Conservative organizations find change to be a very painful process – to be avoided if possible. When people become empowered to start expressing their true feelings the leaders may get uncomfortable. They may think that the people are becoming blasphemous. The ability to identify, surface and confront contradictions is a great feature of Organization

16

Paremiology. Proverbs illustrate this point well, for example, the proverb that says "judge each day, not by its harvest, but by the seeds sown into it."

What may appear as a great blasphemy to the organization may be an opening to a great personal or organizational liberation. When people stop being defensive, they give chance to the truth, and the truth sets us free.

When people come up with seemingly 'blasphemous' ideas, we must have faith in the rationality of the people. We must have faith in the innate goodness which is present in every person. The more we practice this faith and trust, the more we will weaken our tendencies to resist the new.

Tempered ambition

It is only a foolish rooster which believes the sun won't rise if it does not crow

Organization Paremiology challenges organizations to be balanced – to be ambitious and realistic at the same time.

Organizations have a life of their own, which is separate from the lives of the individuals inside them. At the same time, organizations are self-sustaining systems.

For this reason, no individuals are indispensable in a healthy organization. When an individual leaves the organization, the organization will not normally fail to continue to exist. It will live on.

Organization Paremiology emphasizes the importance of organizations' systemic sustainability. As leaders, we should not create a situation where we begin to believe we are indispensable. At the same time, we should not make some members of staff to begin to believe that they are indispensable. We should do our best, but we must all know that the sun will still rise even if we do not crow.

Legacy

The day you die, the wind starts to blow away the marks of your footprints

Organization Paremiology encourages the organization or individuals to think beyond self. It encourages them to think big and long term. While many people are forgotten from the day they die, some people live on long after they are dead. Such people 'literally' refuse to die.

The difference between those who are forgotten and those who are not is the strength of the footprints they leave behind. If you care to immortalize yourself, you can start marking more permanent footprints along your journey of life. What legacy are you creating as an organization? How are you, as an organization, making sure the spirit never dies?

Inclusiveness

Being blind does not mean that one cannot dream or imagine

Respect for all is a key value of Organization Paremiology. Sometimes in organizations, there are people we write off as being incapable of making a meaningful contribution. when they give in their ideas or suggestions, they are not taken seriously.

These people often lack credibility because of their limitations in academic achievement or their backgrounds. Many times when they realize that their suggestions and ideas are not taken seriously, they stop making their contributions and totally lose their confidence.

In getting and using ideas from people we must remember that being blind does not mean one cannot dream or imagine. Sometimes, the lack of visual capacity is compensated by an enlarged capacity to dream and imagine. When we get suggestions and ideas, it is important to look more at the idea than its source. Many times it is difficult to differentiate stupid and brilliant ideas the first time we get them. We may be throwing away many brilliant ideas and entertaining many not so brilliant ideas because we are biased about their source.

Every idea must be scrutinized with objectivity and, if it passes, it must be treated with the seriousness it deserves irrespective of its source.

After all, being 'blind' in organizational settings does not always mean that one will always be blind. People change for the better. Like children in the house, many times we do not notice that they are growing and developing.

Why we need Organization Paremiology

Organizations are formed to solve problems in society. If there were no problems, there would be no need for organizations. In the world today, there are deep and overwhelming problems, such as overpopulation, mass migration, corruption, youth unemployment and terrorism, among others. The level and magnitude of these problems call for a revitalization of most of the organizations we have, and beyond this fact, such problems call for the creation of new organizations. The new organizations will need to be deeper in scope and impact. They need to be more conscious organizations. It is this magnitude and depth that justifies Organization Paremiology.

Effectiveness Organization

Effectiveness Organization had been in existence for 10 years and was helping other organizations improve their organizations. It was a successful organization as more and more organizations came to it for help. But with the passage of time, staff in Effectiveness began to face some problems.

With growth, they began to feel the loss of the 'family feel'. which the organization had before. They had to make appointments to meet each other, they had a lot of paper work to do and too many procedures to follow. This was in addition to increased work per individual. Relationships became tensed up and results began to lose quality. The leaders hired a consultant to help the organization recapture 'the good old' days.

"What you need is to create more space for Grace", the consultant said. He helped the organization to set up a reflection and learning system. The organization agreed to set apart a full day every quarter to reflect on and learn from their practice. On that day, they would not talk about their work as such, but they would reflect on two things and how those two things were affecting their performance.

They would reflect and learn from the following questions:

- What is our understanding of the concept of love in this organization?
- What is our understanding of the concept of Ubuntu in this organization?
- How are we applying this understanding in sustaining healthy work relationships in this organization?
- What is working well? Why?
- What is not working well? Why not?
- What key lessons on improving love and Ubuntu have we learnt?
- How are we going to document and implement these lessons for improved practice?

There are key challenges facing individuals and organizations today. Among these are:

- Globalization of markets and technologies: the market is increasingly being globalized
- Global connectivity – most people with a cellphone have the whole world in their hands. It doesn't really matter where on earth they are now

- Unlimited availability of information – Most of the needed information may be found for free on the internet
- Unprecedented competition – today the world is flat and competition is global

In summary, the context is what Stephen Covey calls 'permanent white water' – a constant, churning, changing environment (2004:105). We need more wisdom to address these challenges better and more effectively. Adopting Organization Paremiology offers a wise choice.

Conclusion

Organization Paremiology builds on the African concept of Ubuntu. The Ubuntu worldview is holistic. In practice, this means that Organization Paremiology takes a systemic view to organization. In this way, Organization Paremiology stands in contrast to many quick-fix organizational improvement efforts. The key tools for Organization Paremiology are parables, metaphors, aspects of (African) culture – Ubuntu and African Proverbs. This book is in two parts. The first part discusses the general and specific principles of Organization Paremiology. The second part discusses the practice of Organization Paremiology.

CHAPTER TWO

Organizational Paremiolgy in Parables

Introduction

Parables are earthly stories with a heavenly or spiritual meaning. The most common parables include the biblical "Prodigal Son", "The Lost Sheep" and the "Lost Coin". Key Biblical Stories also play an equivalent role. Put very simply, a parable is a simple story used in illustrating a moral or spiritual lesson as told by Jesus in the Gospels. A distinctive feature of an African preacher or public speaker, for example, is the stories they tell and how they articulate these stories. A clear example of a story playing the same role is the Exodus in the Old Testament of the Bible. Exodus narrates a story of an 'organization' that was formed to solve a big problem in society – to free an oppressed people. Organizations today are working to free people from different forms of oppression. We can learn so many lessons from the principles of organization in the story of Exodus.

Effective Organization in Exodus

Natural Leadership

> The story of Exodus begins with an undesired situation for the children of Israel – Egyptians made the children of Israel to serve with rigour, and they made their lives bitter with hard bondage, in mortar, and in brick and in all manner of service in the field: all their service, where in they made them serve, was with rigour (Chapter 1: 13 -14).

It was into this situation that Moses, the leader was born. Although he had the privilege to stay with the evil king away from his people, Moses became more and more conscious of his identity and roots as he grew up. He became more and more aware of the situation that his people were going through. He had a natural feeling to help, as seen in the case where he helped a Jew who was fighting an Egyptian. Because Moses had been raised in the king's palace, he had acquired some natural leadership skills. But given the magnitude of the challenge, his leadership preparation and zeal were not sufficient. Moses immediately knew that he did not possess enough power to change the status quo.

The journey begins

Moses' journey to create and manage an 'organization' began with a conscious encounter with God. There was a situation to be resolved. This situation needed God and Moses to work together. God had the power and Moses was to be the instrument through which that power was to be channelled to bring about change. This was the beginning of a conscious leadership journey for Moses. Most great leaders, like Moses, are convinced that they are instruments of the Spirit, and that they are doing work that contributes to the Spirit's grand strategy.

In this encounter, Moses got the assurance of success in the work he was being commissioned to do. He would succeed because the One who was calling him was God himself. And the mission he was going to pursue was God's own –

> ...and I have come down to deliver them out of the land of the Egyptians and to bring them up of the land into a good land and a large, unto a land flowing with milk and honey (Chapter 3:8).

In addition, Moses got the vision and mission of his work. The vision was total end of slavery with the children of Israel moving out of Egypt to a land flowing with milk and honey. His mission was to lead the children of Israel on this journey. His mission was also to channel God's power to fight resistance and bring about....deliverance.

Preparation

After getting the vision and mission, Moses did not rush back to start the work. Because at the time he had become a little older understood the magnitude of the work before him and his own inadequacy. He said, "they will not believe me, nor hearken unto my voice; for they will say, the Lord hath not appeared to thee".

Moses had to be convinced that he now had the spiritual power for leadership, and that this was his main qualification. Change, which all organizations try to bring about, invokes resistance. Resistance is one of the normal reactions to change. If there is no power, the resistance cannot be broken. Another issue in leadership preparation is the reflection on and recognition of one's strength and weakness. Moses said,

> I am not eloquent, neither heretofore, nor since thou has spoken to thy servant; but I am slow of speech, and a slow tongue (Chapter 4: 10).

Natural weaknesses do not stop one from becoming a spiritual leader and leading a spiritual organization. One person's weakness is another person's strength. Moses' weakness was Aaron's strength. Aaron was a good orator.

Moses and Aaron met the people and organized to move out of Egypt –

> and the people believed; and when they heard that the Lord had visited the Children of Israel, and that He had looked upon their affliction, then they bowed their heads and worshipped (Chapter 4: 31).

This was the basis of a spiritual organization – people bound in a shared vision and mission.

The work begins

Work begins with a clear message of what one wants to achieve and a clear strategy on how one intends to achieve those goals. Moses and Aaron told Pharaoh,

> Thus saith the Lord God of Israel, Let my people go that they
> may hold a feast to me in the wilderness (Chapter 5: 1).

Implementation of any strategy will usually invoke resistance. Effective implementation of strategies will require use of power to enforce the strategy. As such, Organizations can use economic power, political power, technological power and socio-cultural power to enforce their strategies against resistance. Moses did not have these powers against the mighty Egypt. He used spiritual power. The strategy involved inflicting Egypt with one plague after another in increasing magnitude until the resistance was defeated and permission was granted to the children of Israel to leave.

Cultivating an effective organization

Identity formation and reorientation are key processes in cultivation of a spiritual organization. The children of Israel had to be physically moved away from the undesired situation towards the desired situation. This helped them to form a new identity as a group of people. It also helped them to have their minds on the vision of a land flowing with milk and honey and away from the slavery days in Egypt. This process was crystallized by miraculously passing through the Red Sea on foot. For the new to be born, the old must die. The ability to kill the past and give birth to the new is a skill that all spiritual leaders need to have. This enables the people to untie their tentacles to the past and release their energies to creating the future which the organization needs. Spirituality involves movement.

Artefacts play an important role in a spiritual organization. Artefacts strengthen the spirit of an organization –

> …and Moses took the bones of Joseph with him: for he had
> strictly sworn the children of Israel, saying God will surely visit
> you; and you shall carry up my bones away hence with you
> (Chapter 13: 19).

Songs play a significant role in consolidating conviction and 'giving space to the Spirit'. Moses and the children of Israel sang a song after crossing the Red Sea. This signified closure with Egypt and a dawn to a new day.

Effective organizations are not heavens. They are faced with challenges just like any other organization. The children of Israel, immediately after crossing the Red Sea, were faced with two problems: lack of fresh water to drink and lack of food. Many times, there will be tests or temptations of the 'old good days'. In one way or another, leaders must be able to provide the basic needs of the followers. An effective organization, is not an organization of saints. It is an organization of imperfect people like any other organization. When there was no water to drink the people chided Moses and said, "Give us water that we may drink...why have you brought us up out of Egypt, to kill us and our children and our cattle with thirst?" The levels of dissonance and disillusionment were very high (Chapter 17: 3).

Documentation

Documentation plays a significant role in an effective organization. Organizational problems do not usually come once in an organization. They will usually come again. If the organization documents how it has resolved a challenge or what it has learned about handling the issues it is facing, it will be better able to handle the challenges when they come again in the future. The children of Israel were confronted by Amalek and a battle ensued. Moses sent troops to fight Amalek while he went up a mount to stand on top of a hill with a rod of God in his hand. This was a two pronged strategy – military and spiritual. And it is important to note that,

> ...it came to pass, when Moses held up his hand, that Israel prevailed; and when he let down his hand, Amalek prevailed (Chapter 17: 11).

This is a deep lesson for spiritual organizations concerning where they draw their power and how. And the Lord spoke to Moses,

> …write this for a memorial in a book, and rehearse it in the ears of Joshua: for I will utterly put out the remembrance of Amalek from under heaven (Chapter 17:14).

External Help

While Moses was fighting a spiritual battle with the rod of God in his hand, there were: times when his hands were heavy (Chapter 17:12). In such instances, Aaron and Hur took a stone and put it under Moses' hands. This is another norm in organisations. Those in leadership might be running out of breath with the vision and strategy. This will require outside or external help to ensure victory in any assignment.

Shared leadership

Shared leadership is a key principle in spiritual organization. Shared work means that no one is over worked and no one is underworked. Moses was handling the people's issues alone every day from morning to evening. Moses' father in law told him:

> The thing that you do is not good. Both you and these people who are with you will surely wear yourselves out. For this thing is too much for you, you are not able to perform it by yourself. Listen now to my voice. I will give you counsel, and God will be with you: Stand before God for the people so that you may bring the difficulties to God. And you shall teach them the statutes and the laws and show them the way in which they must walk and the work they must do. Moreover you shall select from all the people able men, such as fear God, men of truth, hating covetousness and place such over them to be rulers of thousands, rulers of hundreds, rulers of fifties and rulers of tens. And let them judge the people at all times. Then it will be that every great matter they shall bring to you but every small matter they themselves shall judge. So it will be easier with for you, for they will bear the burden with you (Exodus, Chapter 18:17-22).

In effective organizations, people are able to recognize and listen to wisdom. Moses listened to his father in law and became a better leader who could focus on more strategic issues.

Competencies and skills – the effective organization values high skills and competencies. The people elected by Moses to share responsibilities were people of high capabilities for the work they were assigned to do. Shared Values and Principles

Effective organizations are built on shared values and principles. These were encapsulated in the Ten Commandments for the children of Israel. The Ten Commandments became the basis of expected behaviour and peace among the children of Israel. The Ten Commandments contained expectations on behaviour towards God and fellow men.

In addition to the Ten Commandments, there was a 'manual of conduct' spelling out ways to handle different every day human issues like murder, laws of property, personal actions, and the Sabbath (rest). It is important to note that the people were required to rest.

Financial and material sustainability – no organization can survive without money. Self-reliance is key for organizational sustainability.

> And the Lord spake to Moses saying, Speak to the children of Israel saying that they shall bring me an offering: of every man that giveth it willingly with heart you shall take my offering (Chapter 25: 1).

The offerings collected were used to run the 'organization' and implement projects.

Conclusion: Principles of an effective organization

From the story of Exodus, Organization Paremiology teaches us that we can draw the following principles of an effective organization

Vision – the change we want to see as a result of the existence of the organization

Mission – the identity and purpose of the organization – the organization's special and unique contribution.

External Help – Using opportunities and threats facing the organization to the advantage of the organisation.

Shared leadership – the direction the organization is heading to

Shared values and principles – what we believe is important to the organization in pursuing its vision and accomplishing its mission

Implementing strategy – translating the strategies to activities

Crossing the Red Sea – achieving proper closure after dealing with an issue

Artefacts – Objects for strengthening the organizational spirit

Documentation – for organizational memory and future learning
Humility – recognition of the role of the Spirit and others and giving them their rightful space

Financial   self-reliance   –   for   financial   sustainability

CHAPTER THREE

Organizational Paremiolgy in Nature

Introduction

Nature teaches us deep lessons of life. If we heed what nature teaches us, we will be wiser and effective. Organization Paremiology encourages us to be more observant and reflective so that we can be more effective. An example is by observing bees in a beehive as a metaphor of an effective organization. Using a model like this one would play a deeper role in understanding an effective organization and to develop it.

It is important to note, as Gareth (1997) did, that the use of metaphors in organizational improvement efforts, ideas about organization are always based on implicit images or metaphors that persuade us to see, understand, and manage situations in a particular way. Metaphors create insight but they also distort. They have strengths but they also have limitations. In creating ways of seeing, they also create ways of not seeing. Gareth observes that the challenge facing modern managers therefore is to become accomplished in the art of using metaphor to find new ways of seeing, understanding and shaping their actions. The beehive model, as a metaphor, offers them the opportunity to do this.

The Beehive Model

Bees illustrate the most efficient and effective 'organization' in the world (Harrington and Mackin, 2013; Weisz, 1967). Bees live in hives with clear social organization. Each hive has three types of bees, each with distinct work. The queen lays eggs, the male drones fertilize the eggs and the female workers gather food and care for the hive. Each type of bee is adapted for its work. The workers change their duties as their age increases. They start by feeding the larvae; then they ventilate and cool the hive by fanning it with their wings; then they clean the hive and finally they leave on food collecting expeditions. Bees of different ages carry out all these varied tasks at any one time.

The other main duty of worker bees is to attack and, if necessary, sting intruders. When the worker bee uses her sting, her gut is usually ripped out and she dies soon afterwards. Her defence is therefore an act of suicide in which she sacrifices her life for the other bees.

Social ties hold bees in the hive together. The workers lick both the larvae and the queen when they are not busy working. The workers collect food for everyone in the hive. Worker bees that go out to collect food pass on messages to tell the other bees where to find food. They do this by 'dances'. On returning to the hive from the food source, two kinds of dances may be performed. If the food is less than 100m away the bee performs a dance in which it moves round and round in a tight circle telling the other bees food is near but not exactly where to find it. If the food is more than 100m away, another dance is performed which tells the other bees exactly where the food is.

After sharing this model (which is ideal for use in workshops), let people consider their own situation and discuss this first in small groups using the questions below, then encourage the people to share their insights together.

Table 1: Reflection and Learning from the Beehive Model

- What makes bees in a hive an effective organization?
- How similar is this model to our organization?
- How different is it from our organization?
- What could we do differently to be a more effective organization?

What can organizations learn?

1. Products and services

At the crossroads you cannot go in both directions at the same time - African Proverb

Bees produce honey, the sweetest substance on the earth. They also produce wax, another very useful product. The justification of the existence of an organization is determined by how well the organization is serving the people in its task environment. Organizations must first and foremost produce needed products and services which are in their main line of business. This is the only way to ensure the survival of the organization. Organizations must make a lot of effort to consciously and regularly monitor the relevance and competitiveness of their services and products.

Bees produce two products, honey and wax. Organizations must be focused enough to produce as few products/services as possible. It is easier to consolidate an organization's identity and create a brand name when an organization is focused on as a few products/services as possible. When organizations try to do everything, oftentimes, the quality of the services and products is compromised.

An organization's products or services are closely related to its vision. A vision is the gap the organization sees in its task environment. The products or services are a means employed to fill this gap. The products and services must always be seen as a means and not an end in themselves. An organization that is conscious of its vision therefore will take great care to ensure that the products or services it is offering are the best way of realizing its vision.

2. Leadership

What the eyes have seen, the heart cannot forget - African Proverb

When the hive is overcrowded, the queen together with some drones and several thousand workers secede from the colony. The emigrants swarm out to form a new hive. True leaders recognize it when their time is over. They move out to give others a chance.

In the old hive meanwhile, the workers remaining behind raise a small batch of the old queen's eggs. These eggs develop into new queens. The first one to emerge immediately searches out the other queen cells and stings their occupants to death. If it so happens that two queens emerge at the same time, they engage in mortal combat until one remains victorious.

The promotion of flat organizations does not mean doing away with positional leadership. There can only be one legitimate leader at one time e.g. director. Positional leadership must be earned. It must not be given on a silver platter. Organizations must encourage building leadership from within. Bringing in outsiders, while it may have its own advantages, may also have serious disadvantages especially if those inside the organization think that the outsiders are not bringing in any value added which they can bring themselves.

3. Structure

When cobwebs unite, they can tie up a lion - African Proverb

In the hive there are three types of bees, each with different functions. Each type is adapted for its particular job. The division of labor by each type is determined by sex, upbringing and age. The different individuals are accepted and appreciated. Each group in the hive is qualified and experienced and therefore has something to offer to the hive.

Organizations are made up of individuals and teams, and it is the different values, skills and experiences that help the organization to work well. Effective organizations need a mix of people able to work together.

The expectations are very clear in the hive. The drones are expected to fertilize eggs, the queen is expected to lay eggs and the workers are expected to maintain the hive.

Organizations and teams within them will not progress if expectations are not clear. Members must understand and be clear about their roles, responsibilities and what is expected from them. This reduces the risk of conflict and misunderstanding.

4. Relationships

It is better to be surrounded by people than to be surrounded by things - African Proverb

The bees live close together over a long period of time. The bees live together and work together well. With clear division of labour in the hive, no bee is forced to work – they work willingly. In the winter, bees cling together in compact masses. The bees in the centre always work their way out; those on the surface work their way in. A clump of bees thereby withstands freezing, even when exposed to very low temperatures

It may take a long time for people and teams within organizations to work together well. Once this has been achieved, organizations must look at ways in which to consolidate that working environment.

Organizations must have strong internal relationships. They need to work closely together to share and discuss ideas and solutions with all the members contributing.

When conditions get tough, relationships need to become even stronger.

In the hive, there is a high degree of support among members. Workers feed the larvae – the weak members. They also attack, if necessary, sting intruders, sacrificing their lives in the process. They are willing to give up their lives for the well-being of the hive.

People in organizations need to support one another. New members may need a lot of support. Belonging to an organization or teams within the organization may call for sacrifices from the members. Being a member in the organization, individuals may be required to change individual values and behaviour to those needed by the organization as a whole.

Each individual in the organization must take this responsibility to protect the organization from outside forces, which might destroy it. Individuals need to be committed to the organization's purpose and to one another. This commitment is the force that bonds the individuals together.

When they come back from their food expeditions successfully, the workers perform dances. Organizations will not be successful without effective communication. Open communication builds trust. Organizations need access to information so that individuals and teams can manage themselves. Individuals in organizations need to listen to each other as communication is seen to have taken place only when the receiver has exactly received what was being communicated.

Successful organizations are fun. Dancing is a sign of celebration, happiness and fun. Individuals get a lot of satisfaction by being part of the organization and may openly express excitement, enthusiasm and enjoyment while carrying out their roles and tasks.

Every time the workers come back from food expeditions, they call for a 'meeting' to give feedback of the success of the trip. Frequent and regular meetings play a critical role in the success of organizations. People in organizations must physically meet and update each other about developments in relation to the task. After the 'meetings' the bees go out together to get the food. Effective organizations get the work done.

5. Self-Development

The poorest person is not one without money but the one without a vision - African Proverb

In the six months or so of its life, a worker bee does not perform the same duties continually. The age of the bee determines the kind of work it can do; the young bees perform housekeeping tasks, the older ones make food collection trips. The middle-aged bees spend their time feeding the queen and the younger bees.

Individuals in organizations must grow and develop. As they grow and develop in their skills and competencies, so must their responsibilities. Flexibility in organizations is a great asset. Varied activities make life more exciting. Organizations and teams that offer little variety may soon lose their appeal.

Bees have clear and meaningful work – producing eggs, caring for the larvae and maintaining the hive. Likewise, organizations need a good balance between task achievement and maintaining or building up organizational members.

It is also important that individuals must benefit from belonging to the organization. They should gain more than they put into the organization. Individuals must see added value to their efforts in the organization.

6. Sustainability and efficient use of resources

It is not money that builds a house; it is wisdom - African Proverb

The workers ensure that the hive has all the practical resources it needs to perform well. The bees that go to collect food gather nectar, which is turned to honey in the hive. The honey is sealed in wax in preparation for winter when there aren't as many flowers to provide nectar.

Organizations must not only think about their short term but also their long-term resource needs. They should consciously seek to become self-reliant in the long term. This is the essence of organizational sustainability.

When winter is approaching all the drones are expelled from the colony. Not contributing to the wellbeing of the population makes males merely use up food, which is at premium in the cold season.

In addition to acquiring more resources, organizations must seek to make efficient use of the resources they already have. Many organizations do not maximize the use of the resources they have. There is a lot of waste. A good example is in IT. Many organizations, for example, use the computer only as a typewriter and adding machine.

7. Relationships with stakeholders

One man cannot move a mountain - African Proverb

Bees have mutually benefiting relationships with stakeholders. While they take nectar from flowers they simultaneously aid in the pollination process of the plants.

Organizations must seek to add value to any relationship that they commit to and at the same time they must see that all the relationships they get involved in are adding and not taking away value from them. This is the principle of synergy. Any relationship not adding value is not worthy maintaining.

Conclusion

Metaphors help to simplify the explanation of complex phenomena such as organizations. This chapter has discussed some of the most critical organizational success factors we can learn from bees in a hive. Aided by some African proverbs, which are metaphors in themselves, the chapter has discussed the following factors:

- Focus and concentration
- Leadership
- Structure
- Internal relationships
- Self-development

- Sustainability
- Relationships with stakeholders

Just like any other model, this one has limitations. A major limitation of the model is that all the activities in the hive are instinctual and not conscious. Coincidentally, this is a similar limitation in many organizations. Organizational consciousness is low in many organizations. This is a major explanation why people in organizations spend more energy in improving programmes and activities as compared to addressing organizational issues holistically. While instinct may be sufficient for bees, organizations that are not consciously improving themselves cannot be effective and sustainable in the long term.

Despite its other limitations, we can learn much from bees and the model may prove very useful. Try to apply it to your own organization using the discussion questions.

CHAPTER FOUR

Organization Paremiology in Ubuntu

Introduction

Organization Paremiology is based on the African cultural heritage of Ubuntu. African cultural heritage, which was passed on from generation to generation, has been a source of guidance for communities in times of peace, uncertainty, birth, life and death. At its best, it has been the basis for identity, respect and self-confidence. It has enabled the people to live in harmony with the physical, social and spiritual environments. It provides the foundation for leadership, problem solving, decision making and hope for the future. This is the essence of African culture built on Ubuntu and Love. Ubuntu is built on five interrelated principles:

- Sharing and collective ownership of responsibilities and challenges
- The importance of people and relationships over things
- Participatory decision making and leadership
- Loyalty; and
- Reconciliation as a goal of conflict management and resolution

It is around these five principles that African communities were organized for sustenance and empowerment. These principles can be used to develop a model for a modern spiritual organization.

1. Taking collective responsibility for the organization

Ants united can carry a dead elephant to their cave

Collective responsibility is key to organizational success. In many organizations, both leaders and followers blame each other, thereby abdicating their responsibility. Blaming others for organizational challenges can dissipate the organization's energy and diminish its ability to address the challenges.

Collective responsibility also applies to the fair distribution of benefits and efforts. When some people are perceived as unjustifiably benefiting more than others from the organization's collective efforts, this will lead to resentment and strained relationships, adversely affecting team spirit and organizational performance. In addition, people must feel that others are pulling their weight in the organization. When people feel that they are 'selling more than they are buying', they may reduce their efforts or opt out. This can kill the hard working and innovative spirit in the organization.

Collective responsibility requires a collectively shared vision for the organization. Vision means the sense of focus and the change the organization wants to bring about in society.

2. Importance of relationships

When spider webs unite they can tie up a lion

The Ubuntu emphasis on relationships may usefully be applied to leadership. Organizations can be viewed as extended families in which relationships are close enough to go beyond the professional level. In formal organizations, there is a tendency to not cross the boundary or interfere with other people's personal lives outside the organization. This is despite the fact that what is done outside the office affects staff eventually and the organization as well.

In the African context, it may be more appropriate to create an organizational environment where people feel, but are also enabled to 'interfere in the other people's lives' if they feel it would benefit the person and the organization.

3. Participatory Leadership

Leadership development needs to emphasise the importance of involving people, through meaningful participation, in addressing the challenges the organization is facing. When people participate meaningfully, they will also own and commit to the identified solutions. In addition, their sense of belonging to the organization is enhanced.

Individual leaders should not be allowed to become too powerful. The important role of the board of trustees is to provide checks and balances in the organization. This is done primarily by ensuring that the organization has effective policies and procedures that are actually adhered to.

Policies, systems and procedures

If you want to go fast go alone. If you want to go far, go with others

It is right for a goat to bite the dog, but it is wrong for the goat to bite the dog

Policies ensure consistency in decision making in an organization. They also ensure fairness in the treatment of people. Perceived unfairness is detrimental to organizational effectiveness. Morale is destroyed when employees feel that there is favouritism in the organization.

In some organizations, the policies, systems and procedures apply only to certain categories or groups of employees and not to others. The good side of the policies is applied to others, while the punitive side is applied to others. The question then is: how are policy processes supposed to be implemented? Are they being practiced fairly across the whole organization? Do we know how fair the staff rate the organization to be?

Policies often arise out of experience. At the beginning of the organization we are usually informal and operate as a family. As the organization develops however, a need for more order arises. This leads to the need for policies to aid in consistent decision making.

Determining which policies to implement comes out of the experiences the organization may meet. When formulating a new policy, it is important that all interests are taken into account. The interests of all the people in the organization and also the interests of the future organization. This requires the people who formulate the policies to be sober and rational.

In the case, for example, where an employee bashes an official vehicle and there is a policy issued soon afterwards that drivers, not employees, should drive all the official vehicles, we may soon regret the decision when we see the cost implications of the decision.

Consideration should be made on, among others, does your organization have clear guidelines for expected behaviour, and rewards and punishments associated with these guidelines? Are they documented?

Structure – how roles and responsibilities are shared within and among organizations

Many hands make work lighter
A cat in his house has the teeth of a lion

An effective organization strives towards an organizational structure that is organic. This is characterized by:

- Being 'flat' and people working mostly through teams. It is an organization of 'equals'.
- The organization is responsive to the changing needs in the environment and
- Redefined and clear roles and responsibilities
- Roles and responsibilities are temporary and may change from time to time
- Individuals and departments collaborate
- Problems are solved by task forces composed of diverse professional skills
- The organization collaborates with other stakeholders
- There are conscious team building efforts to ensure close and satisfying relationships.

4. **Loyalty**

The river that forgets its source will soon dry up

The Ubuntu concept of loyalty means that organizational interests must always precede personal interest. Many leaders in organizations sacrifice long term organizational interests for short term self-interests. Leadership must be taken as an opportunity to serve rather than a means to accumulate personal wealth and power.

No person should be more important than the organization, no matter how much the person is loved or hated. When a leader's continued existence in the organization becomes a danger to its survival or well-being, the leader may need to be fired or they may be asked to resign.

Organizations should also encourage in their staff a culture of pride in the organization. In many organizations, staff feel that there are better organizations out there and therefore they do not make much commitment to their own. Managing the culture and performance of the organization helps leaders to develop pride among staff. True commitment to an organization is based on people deeply and consciously connecting their values and those of the organization, so it is important to identify these personal values and link them to those of the organizational culture.

Culture

Organizational culture comprises the norms and values practiced by an organization, and how these are helping or hindering the organization's ways of being, ways of doing and ways of relating with others.

An organization is built primarily on a set of agreed and shared values. A key distinguishing feature of an effective organization is faith in these values. This faith is expressed in action, not mere words. This is active faith, not passive or lazy faith. Sustaining this faith requires a lot of energy and consciousness.

A river does not run straight because there was no one to advise it

When I graduated from college, I worked with the government as a field research assistant. I was given a group of technicians to administer a questionnaire among respondents in rural areas.

One day, when I went to supervise the group, I found that they had packed the project vehicle with firewood from a nearby forest. Instead of working, they were transferring the firewood to their homes. I got angry and rebuked them.

When my supervisor came, the technicians reported the matter to him. Surprisingly, they reported the matter fairly and objectively. To my surprise, my supervisor apologized on my behalf in my presence. She actually said, "Forgive him, he is just coming from college".

What I later learned was that this was a deep-rooted culture and even my supervisor was caught up in it. It had taken so long to develop and it was not easy to break it.

Organizational culture refers to the way we do our things. In this organization. Culture can be:

- Empowering or disempowering
- Flexible/rigid
- Future oriented/past oriented
- Inward/outward looking
- People centered/things centered
- Project centered /learning centered
- Liberating or fearful organization
- Open/closed culture
- Democratic/autocratic
- Accommodating/exclusive

An organizational leadership can embed organizational culture through different mechanisms. According to Schein (2010), these include both primary and secondary mechanisms:

Primary mechanisms

- What leaders pay attention to, measure, and control on a regular basis
- How leaders react to critical incidents and organizational crises
- How leaders allocate resources
- Deliberate role modelling
- How leaders allocate rewards and status
- How leaders recruit, select, promote and excommunicate

Secondary mechanisms

- Organizational design and structure
- Organizational systems and procedures
- Rites and rituals of the organization
- Design and physical space, facades and buildings
- Stories about important events and people
- Formal statements of organizational philosophy, creeds and charters

Values

Character is like a pregnancy; you cannot hide it for long

A key value for spiritual organizations is integrity

There is nothing as powerful as exemplary leadership. We are stronger if there is no gap between what we say and what we do. If we raise our moral grounds upon which we can execute tough decisions, people can testify to our walking the talk.

Leaders set the tone. Consciously or unconsciously, the people we lead will follow our example. When the leader limps, the followers limp too. Do we honestly want the people we lead to become like us? We must work at developing our integrity and character. When we develop these at personal level, we will also be developing the organization's integrity and character.

We must become models of hard work, honesty, selflessness and character. The more we are models, the more we will increase the effectiveness of our organizations.

Consider the following story on the value of importance of honesty and integrity;

In a village, the elders met at the end of each month to discuss issues affecting the village. For the meeting, each elder brought a calabash of wine which they poured into one pot and shared or drank together while they were discussing their issues.

One day, one elder decided to bring water in his calabash and not wine, hoping that the others would not notice.

Unfortunately, on that particular day, all the elders thought the same way. They brought water instead of wine hoping that the others would not notice.

It was time to start drinking the wine – they were all so ashamed.

Valuing sensitivity

No matter how often a man quarrels with his wife, he does not do in the hours leading to bed time

One of the most difficult things we have to deal with in organizational life is to deal with sensitive issues. This may involve resolving conflicts, following up on allegations of fraud or sexual harassment and many others. These are the type of issues that if we are given a chance, we would avoid.

One of the key success factors in handling such matters is the timing. If we are wrong at timing, we may do more damage to the people involved, as a result, Organizational effectiveness may suffer. If we are right in our timing, we may help the people involved and the organization more.

Instead of handling sensitive matters first thing in the morning consider handling them as the last thing of the day. This helps the person to think through the discussion over night after the meeting. Consider again discussing the issue on a Friday rather than Monday so that the person has the whole weekend to think through rather than spoil his or her work for the whole week.

Creating a balance between being visionary and being grounded

Different people have different orientations. Others are futuristic and visionary while others are more pragmatic and practical. When the organization is skewed towards one direction, it suffers. There must be a balance. Those who are pragmatic need to be inspired by those who are visionary. Those who are visionary need to be pulled down to the ground by those who are more pragmatic and practical.

At a personal level, we need to become aware of our orientation. When we know our orientation, we know our strengths and weaknesses. If we are visionary oriented, our strengths is in creating the ideal picture and our challenge may be to translate the picture into practice.

As we discover our strengths and weaknesses, that is the first step in addressing our challenges. The weaknesses show the areas that may need addressing to improve ourselves.

We must aim at being balanced. We must look at the sky but at the same time discover the gems in the ground.

5. Reconciliation

Unity among cattle makes the lion lie down hungry

The organizational mechanisms for conflict resolution must aim at fairness, trust, reconciliation and the building of trust . People should have the right to appeal to higher levels, if they are not satisfied with the outcome of the conflict resolution process. These should be clearly and spelt out and be made know to all employees.

The aim of conflict resolution must be to help the people involved reach an agreement by consensus, rather than forcing them to 'shake hands' before they feel that the issues have been resolved or justice has been administered. Giving and receiving forgiveness must provide the foundation for relationship building.

In a conflict situation involving a subordinate and superior, great wisdom and discretion should be exercised to balance fairness, maintain respect and avoid loss of face in case of the superior party being in the wrong.

In case of simple conflicts, leaders should delegate conflict management, and encourage people to resolve these conflicts at as low a level as possible. This gives people in higher positions more space and time to get involved in bigger and more strategic issues.

Everything is interrelated

A farmer bought a rat trap and brought it home. When the rat saw the trap, he went to the chicken to ask for help. "Please help me, myself and my family we are in danger because of the trap the farmer has put in the house. Please can you help me by removing the trap?" The chicken said, "that is not my problem. In addition, I am busy with my own problems". Disappointed, the rat went to the goat. The goat said he was busy and this was not his problem. Not giving up, the rat went to the cow. The cow said the same thing. The rat came back disappointed.

A few days later, an incident happened. The farmer was bitten by a poisonous snake which was mistakenly caught on the rat trap. A herbalist came to try to cure him. The herbalist said the broth of a chicken is an effective medicine for snakebites. The chicken was killed to provide medicine. Unfortunately, this medicine did not work. The farmer's illness was getting worse. Relatives came from far and wide to do a vigil. They needed to eat good food. They killed the goat.

The illness got even worse, the farmer unfortunately died. For the funeral ceremony they killed the cow.

Conclusion

Organization Paremiology is built on the African heritage of Ubuntu. Ubuntu is rooted in the five key values of:

- Sharing and collective ownership of responsibilities and challenges
- The importance of people and relationships over things
- Participatory decision making and leadership
- Loyalty; and
- Reconciliation as a goal of conflict

Based on the above, Organization Paremiology places great emphasis on the interconnected and systemic nature of organizations.

CHAPTER FIVE

Organizationnal Paremiology in African Proverbs

The essence of Organization Paremiology is in African proverbs. By using African proverbs, Organization Paremiology simplifies, deepens and clarifies the otherwise relatively complex subject of Organization Development or Organization Capacity Development. Proverbs are an integral part of African culture. They are simple statements with deep meaning, serving as guidelines for individual, family, community and village behaviour, as built upon repeated real life experiences and observation over time. For example, a proverb like "if the sun says it is more powerful than the moon then let it come and shine at night" speaks about the importance of respecting roles and responsibilities in organizations. "The river that forgets its source will soon dry up" talks about the importance of values in an organization. One good proverb can explain adequately what a classic Organization Development Book requires a chapter to do.

Direction and Focus

How will you be remembered?

You can only jump over a ditch if you see it from afar

Cultivating a personal sense of vision and mission enables individuals to be intentional about the contribution they want to make and the legacy they want to leave behind. It helps one to set one's priorities in order. Maxwell (2008:248) reports the results of a study that was conducted with people who were over the age of 95. They were asked the following question: "if you could live your life over again, what would you do differently?" Three main themes consistently emerged from their responses:

If I had it to do over again, I would reflect more.
If I had it to do over again, I would risk it.
If I had to do it over again, I would do more things that would live on after I am dead.

These themes provide deep wisdom to those who are at the stage in their life to put them into practice.

How is your success affecting you?

Those who the gods want to send first they send important visitors.

Success attracts recognition and admirers. While this is good and satisfying, it may also pose a big danger. Handling success is as difficult as creating it. A woman of a very successful local community agriculture development initiative had this to say:

> When we became successful, we began to receive visitors one after another. We started getting invitations and to national and international conferences. In the process our work suffered. We worked less and less. The other time I came back from an international conference and we found all the pigs dead.

It is important to ensure the way we handle visitors who come to learn from us and admire our success, and how we handle invitations we get so that these do not harm our personal effectiveness or that of our organization.

Do you know that your organization can be the best for you in the whole world?

A happy man marries the woman he loves; a happier man loves a woman he marries.

Many people are not satisfied with the organization they work for. They believe that some other organizations out there are better than theirs. Many times they are attracted by higher remuneration or better benefits offered by the other organizations.

What we see from a distance may however not be a full truth about the organizations we admire. Each organization has its own problems and challenges. Each organization has its light and shadow. Moving to another organization in search of a perfect organization may lead to disillusionment.

Instead of running away, we must make efforts to transfer our own to the organization we want it to be. If we manage to do this, we will be more satisfied than if we were to go and enjoy the freedom that somebody else's intelligence and hard work had created.

Culture and values

How open-minded are you?

Truth is truth irrespective of the source

It doesn't matter whether the cat is black or white, as long as it catches the mouse

Sometimes our key to breakthrough as an individual or an organization is found in the most unlikely places or with the most unlikely person. Our minds have been conditioned to expect good things from certain places and certain people, and this may close us off from some opportunities.

How open minded are we when we listen to people we do not expect to offer much to us, or when we visit places where we believe we cannot do much business? When seeking ideas in an organization, do we only go to those in senior positions? When junior staff or volunteers bring their ideas, do we accommodate them or pay no attention to them?

It requires conscious effort and humility to open our minds to the possibility that our personal and organizational lives can be forever changed by an idea of a humble 'tea-server' in the organization. We need to objectively look at the quality of the ideas and not necessarily the people who offer them.

What drives you?

If money grew on trees, many people would be married to monkeys.

Individuals and organizations need money to survive, grow and prosper.

Profit, however, is not a goal but a product of good management and leadership. Seen from another angle, money is a means toward an end. It is not an end in itself. It is a means toward the accomplishment of the organization's mission.

Many organizations would do anything just to get money. Some non-profit organizations will forget their vision to get 'easy' donor money that has no relationship whatsoever with their vision or mission. Some businesses will cut corners or use shortcuts to enhance profits.

It is always important to base our actions concerning money on our values and our identity -what we want to be known for. As individuals and organizations, we must identify a core set of shared values, bring them to consciousness and practically live them every day. There must be systems to reinforce the values, and we should not depart from them. Money and profits built on a shared set of values are truly sustainable. We must be driven by values.

Strategy

What is the basis for assessing the health of your organization?

Each new day is the first day of the rest of your lives.

If you were perfect yesterday, it does not mean that you are also perfect today. What we were yesterday is not necessarily the same as what we are today. What was adequate for addressing yesterday's problems may not be for today's problems.

Every system has a tendency toward entropy or breaking down unless it is maintained and natured. Individuals and organizations too, being living systems, have a tendency toward breaking down unless they are maintained and nurtured. Sometimes, the most dangerous moments in a person's life come when that person has just been declared 'successful' for that moment. They may become complacent.

We must have an individual and organizational 'check-up' each year. This helps us to identify our strengths and weaknesses objectively. Based on the assessment, we can undertake the right action to ensure effectiveness.

What are you clinging to?

Throw away what you don't need.

When carrying out personal or organizational activities, we may form attachments to them. As time goes by, most of the activities we are engaged in become obsolete. As the organization must move into the future, we need to throw away every activity that holds it to its yesterday.

As the environment changes and the needs of the organization, individuals, or clients change, each activity that stops yielding results must not deter our commitment to move forward into the future to which we aspire.

What activities are we currently implementing in the organization or our personal lives? How long have we been implementing these activities? What is the justification for continuing to implement them? Should we abandon some of them?

How thorough are you in your implementation?

A hunter with one arrow does not shoot with a careless aim.

It is important to do one thing and do it thoroughly, rather than jumping to so many activities at the same time. The ability to focus and maintain the focus is a strength and a key factor for individual and organizational effectiveness.

Many individuals and organizations are tempted to implement a few more projects because of opportunities in their task environment, while not giving thought to their capacity to deliver. When we do not have the capacity to deliver or the capacity to implement the projects, we are forced to take short cuts. The problem with short cuts is that they damage the quality and impact of the service. Customers and clients will not be impressed. At the end of the day, the individual or the organization suffers.

Reflection and learning

How deep are your solutions?

A bee sting can only be removed by uprooting it.

What we see on the surface as problems are usually just symptoms of deeper underlying problems. If we only deal with the symptoms without addressing the underlying causes, the problem will keep coming back in more devastating ways.

A problem of inadequate funding may be solved by writing more funding proposals. A drop in profits may be addressed by strengthening the marketing section of the organization and enhancing the service or product quality. In the case of inadequate funding the root cause of the problem may be lack of skills and competences in writing high quality proposals or in effective or ineffective financial policies, systems and procedures. Unless these deeper problems are addressed, any surface solution will not bring about lasting change.

As an individual or organization, we need to take time to identify the problems we are experiencing. We need to dig deeper beyond what we see on the surface until we identify the root causes of the problems. We must address our problems at this level for lasting solutions.

When do you celebrate success?

A person who is putting on his Armor for war should not boast like the one who is taking it off.

Don't laugh at the fallen ones when you are still standing on slippery grounds.

A truly happy person is the one who has served an organization and is retiring or quitting after realising personal and organizational goals. Such a person has every reason to celebrate. The right time to boast, therefore, is when we are taking off the Armor.

The person who is just putting on Armor cannot be completely sure because there are so many slain giants on the battlefield. The best one can do is to take into account all of the factors that are within one's control and do one's best. One should still aim for the sky, but the outcome is not entirely under the individual's control.

As we are doing our work, let us hold on until the end so that we can also boast after the successful completion of our contribution to the organization's life. Let us avoid anything that would keep us from a happy ending.

Competition

How well informed are we about the strength of our competition?

It was ignorance that made the rat challenge the cat to a wrestling match.

Many times we get a brilliant idea and we want to immediately rush to the market with it. Before such a rush, it is important to assess the current and potential competition and its strength. It is important to do this by considering such questions as:

- Do we have enough material and monetary resources to sustain the business?
- Do we understand where this service or product will fit in the market?
- Do we have enough capacity to compete favourably on quality and service?

It is always important to be realistic about our capabilities and the realities of the task environment we will be working on.

- Thinking strategically-challenging assumptions and studying trends and patterns.
- Creating a long-term vision for the organisation.
- Understanding the strengths of the competition.
- Identifying and changing organizational core competencies like quality, speed, flexibility, expertise, and capacity to innovate.

How proactive are you?

The pasture does not go to the cow but it is the cow that goes to the pasture.

> There is the saying that 'he who waits, waits forever.' We all want good things to happen to us but good things will not happen to us. We have to make them happen. We have to go after what we want, rather than waiting for the good things to come to us.

We attract good things into our lives and our organizations by spending our time doing something useful. Enrol in a correspondence course, attend a motivational seminar, read books, seek advice. Join a professional club, etc. Make sure your time is spent usefully and productively at all times. If we do not get what we want in our personal and organizational lives, it is often because we are doing something wrong or we are not doing enough. Don't just sit there. Do something. When we do something, we will become someone.

Personal Mastery

How strongly do you want to succeed?

Determination pays, the sparrow married a pigeon.

Many times, we fail to get what we want not because we do not want it, but because we do not want it badly enough. Somehow, we have created a comfort zone with our achievements from the past. We mistake wanting to achieve our goals for wishing we had what we want. As individuals or organizations, we must have a red-hot desire that is all compelling in order to achieve what we truly care about. The desire must be so strong that it literally drives us to the desired goal. It is this type of desire that overcomes every obstacle on the way. Determination starts with creating an inspiring vision of the ideal being sought. After the vision, one must create a challenging goal in each of the major roles one plays in life and set a step by step activity plan to achieve the goals with clear indicators.

We must also get advice from those who have already walked on similar journeys and succeeded. These are the people who can prove what they say by their lives and not just by words.

Lastly, we must make it a point to be first class in everything we do, to be as good as the best in the world - if not better.

How well are you managing your good times?

Wealth is like a rat's tail, it easily slips away

Sometimes we find ourselves in an unbelievable situation where we experience no financial limitation at all. As an individual or organization we have all the money we need and more. Such situations, however, usually do not last long. They are temporary. We should therefore not be tempted to think that things will always be like that. To make sure we will find ourselves in such a lucky and enviable situation, we must make investment plans that will act as 'shock absorbers' to us as organizations and individuals, and as we move into the unpredictable future.

Extra money for an individual or in an organization is not for wasting. It is for future preparedness. If we squander today's extra money, we may find that tomorrow we have no experience in short-lived glory. Yesterday's excess may create tomorrow's deficit. Yesterday's millionaires have become today's beggars because of financial mismanagement.

How wide is your scope?

If you live in a small house you may think you have a lot of furniture.

A small house does not have much space. It is therefore easily filled. When we live in a small house, we may think we have a lot of property. If we move to a big house, we are often surprised to see how little or few our belongings are.

When our mental scope as individuals and organizations is small, we are often satisfied. We have no motivation to keep stretching ourselves. To get inspired to move on, we must stretch our horizons. When we have more 'mental space' we soon discover how little our assets really are. It is this dissatisfaction that drives us to seek and become more.

What comes first, your talking or thinking?

A word spoken cannot be called back.

The wounds caused by words are painful and take long to heal than physical wounds. For this reason, you must always be careful what you say to other people. It is better to say nothing at all than to hurt people with your words. The times when we are likely to say things that will hurt other people are when we are angry or disappointed. Anger and disappointment cloud out our sense of judgement and rationality. When we go ahead and speak in this state, we usually regret what we said. When we sense that we are angry or disappointed, it is wise to withhold our words and wait until we have cooled and are sober. When we are in our normal state, let our words be few but powerful.

Relationships

How are you treating new and young employees in the organization?

You can straighten a tree when it is young.

Young and new employees must be moulded into the culture of the organization. This is often a tough process for many, because it may involve a breaking down remodelling process. When we watch movies concerning a trainee, a mentor in martial arts, the relationship can teach a lot of lessons. The film usually portrays a young, naïve, over-confident young person who is slowly broken down by the elderly mentor, but at the same time moulded into a more effective person. It is never an easy process for the trainee but in the end they appreciate it. In order to ensure the future survival of an organization, we need young people who are young and developing to replace us when we are going. These individuals must be at least as good as we are, and preferably better. The only way to ensure this is to create such a crop of people through appropriate mentoring and coaching.

How healthy are your relationships in the organization?

Living close to each other does not mean you are relating well.

Relationship problems are big in organizations. Many organizations do not take conscious efforts to build healthy relationships among their people, and this leads to alienation and conflicts in the organization.

As long as people are not fighting or arguing, leaders may not see it as their duty to encourage and facilitate relationship building in organizations. The best time to build relationships is before they go sour. Prevention is always better than cure.

Relationships must be built among individuals, between departments and within the centre in the entire organisation. It is only that which is rating well within itself that can relate well with other organizations and stakeholders. The more we do these type of things, the better the organization that we have.

In addition, organizations also need proper and effective grievance and conflict resolutions and procedures. People must feel that the organization genuinely cares for them and about their grievances.

Leadership development

How courageous are you?

Avoiding a fight is not cowardice

It is wisdom not to engage in a losing battle. When we have assessed the situation and concluded that our chances of winning are slim, it is wise to pull out of the race. It does not help to go on knowing that we cannot win. When we go into losing battles, we waste resources of time, money and energy. It is bad for morale. The more we lose, the more we doubt our capacities and the more we lose our self-confidence.

We must only run in winnable races. When we do this, we build ourselves up. We get more resources. We get more self-confident and we are ready to engage in bigger and bigger fights. We must begin small and grow big over time rather than begin big and be pushed back to where we belong because we were unrealistic or over ambitious.

How much pain do you have in your organization?

Tears never flow in the house of a coward

A struggle without casualties is not a struggle

Development is a breakthrough to a new level of being, doing and relating. It is a breakthrough to a new level of existence. Any breakthrough is preceded by a crisis.

A crisis signifies pain. Without pain there can be no development. If all we have in our organizations are good times, chances are we are stuck. If development is happening, we must experience some pain along the way.

Are we avoiding pain in our organization? By avoiding pain, we may be holding the organization from experiencing breakthroughs to a new level and higher levels of effectiveness. We should not look for pain, but when it comes, let us celebrate the development opportunity it will precipitate if we handle it well.

> The attitude must be that, if we take an approach that is good, it is not by accident; that everyone and everything which shows up in our life is there for a reason; and that we are moving toward our ultimate destiny for learning, growth and achievement, we will begin to see every event – no matter how difficult or challenging – as a chance for enrichment and advancement in our life (Canfied, 2007:75).

How strong are your lenses?

From a distance a lion looks like a baboon

Many times people do not tell the truth. We have to establish the truth ourselves. When people offer us deals, they may show us only the good side. They may not show us the full cost of what we are paying.

When we receive financial and narrative reports, do we read between the lines? We should not put too much trust in people. We should not trust other people more than we trust ourselves. At the end of the day, the final responsibility lies with ourselves. We are the ones to deal with the consequences of our decisions and actions or inactions.

We must develop the capacity for critique. We must develop the capacity for keen observation. We must always understand that not all that glitters is gold.

How deep is your leadership?

Still waters run deep

Along the path of growth and development, each individual or organization will meet some crisis. The natural instinct when a crisis hits is to panic. When people panic, they lose objectivity and become powerless.

The real strength of a leader is manifested in times of crisis. Real leaders are invisible until a crisis hits. A leader who runs away, abandoning his people, is not a real leader. While everyone is panicking the real leader remains calm. He or she is not shaken but rather strengthened by the crisis. He or she draws from the depth of his or her leadership to calm the storm. Let a crisis hit an organization and you will know how real the leaders are.

Conclusion

In this chapter I have presented some insights from my own experience using African Proverbs as material for contemplation. As an Organizational Paremiologist, I have found that African proverbs are key for organizational learning. They contain deep insight that can enable individuals and organizations to identify, surface and confront their contradictions or shadows for deeper and lasting change. A single proverb may produce a deeper insight than an entire contemporary management book.

African proverbs speak much more deeply to individuals and organizations because they communicate at the level of being and relationship. In this sense African proverbs are soulful and facilitative to spiritual growth and development for individuals and organizations.

CHAPTER SIX

Summary of Key Principles of Organization Paremiology

Introduction

Organization Paremiology helps improve organizational performance and effectiveness by using parables, metaphors, aspects of African culture (Ubuntu) and African Proverbs as tools for reflection to draw insight for organizational effectiveness. The reflection focuses on the key organizational components. These are summarized below, as follows:

Vision – the change we want to see as a result of the existence of the organization, Organization Paremiology helps organizations to clarify the change they want to see in the world. Organization Paremiology aims to lift organizational aspirations beyond mere selfish ones by demonstrating that organizations are actually spiritual entities serving more noble purposes.

Mission – the identity and purpose of the organization - Organization Paremiology helps organizations to clarify the unique contribution of their existence. It helps people in the organization to see that there is not just work but a mission. Organization Paremiology aims at bringing out the true meaning of purpose in work.

Shared leadership – the direction the organization is heading – Organization Paremiology believes every person is a leader. Proverbs like "if the sun says it is more powerful than the moon, then let it come and shine at night" illustrate the point well.

Shared values – what we believe is important to the organization in pursuing its vision and accomplishing its mission -

Organization Paremiology is based on the five values of Ubuntu:

- Sharing and collective ownership of responsibilities and challenges
- The importance of people and relationships over things
- Participatory decision making and leadership
- Loyalty; and
- Reconciliation as a goal of conflict management and resolution

Implementing strategy – translating the strategies to activities. Formulating good strategies is difficult, Implementing the strategies is even more difficult. Most organizations suffer from an execution gap. Organization Paremiology aims at supporting the organization to more consciously formulate and implement their strategies.

"Crossing the Red Sea" – achieving proper closure after dealing with an issue. This talks about learning from major changes - positive or negative. It talks about avoiding being stuck in the old good days and the 'hell of yesterday' and moving forward to the future we want.

Artefacts – Objects for strengthening the spirit – Organization Paremiology encourages a conscious use of artefacts. The parables, the metaphors, aspects of African culture and the proverbs may be used as artefacts.

Documentation – for organizational memory and future learning – Organization Paremiology demonstrates a change from a purely oral culture to a culture emphasising memory as a tool for learning. In this, the culture of documentation is emphasised. Proverbs like "the weakest ink is stronger than the mightiest memory" illustrate this point well.

Humility – recognition of the role of the Spirit and others and giving them their rightful space - Organization Paremiology emphasises the holistic nature of organization development by recognizing that everything is related to everything and gives sensitivity to this.

Financial self-reliance – for financial sustainability – reducing dependence and increasing self-reliance is a key value for Organization Paremiology. It also emphasizes the inter dependence of organizations. A proverb like "ants united can carry a dead elephant to their cave" illustrate the point well.

A summary of the key principles of Organization Paremiology

A summary of key principles of Organization Paremiology is given below:

1. Speaking to people's realities – parables, metaphors, culture, proverbs and folktales come from the people's realities. They come from what the people have experienced again and again over a very long period of time. These are like the theorems in mathematics. They are established truths, and we will only do ourselves harm if we do not heed them.
2. Using the most relevant tools for the situation – this talks about the power of communication and its relevance. Organization Paremiology is organized around the stages of life. There are folktales and proverbs for children, adolescents, young adults and adults. There are also proverbs and folktales for different contexts. Organization Paremiology emphasises the use of the most relevant parable, metaphor, aspect of culture, proverb, folktale and indeed any other tool as deemed appropriate.
3. Organization Paremiology emphasises the importance of discretion. This involves the ability to discern when the use of any of the tools of Organization Paremiology may be unnecessary, or indeed harmful.

4. Dealing with contradictions and confronting shadows – one of the biggest strengths of Organization Paremiology is its ability to challenge and deal with contradiction while minimizing tension. A proverb like "Judge each day not by its harvest but by the seeds you sow into it" illustrates this point very well.

5. Human Dignity – Organization Paremiology aims at promoting and preserving human dignity and respect by praising the good and discouraging the bad. The good person will always end up the winner. The bad person will end up the loser. Respect for the individual and the group are primary values of Organization Paremiology.

6. Everything is related – Organization Paremiology teaches that life is one indivisible whole. What happens in one part affects the other parts. It teaches that life is a boomerang both in the short and long term and, by so doing, encourages us to live by love always.

CHAPTER SEVEN

The Practice of Organization Paremiology

Introduction

The practice of Paremiology dwells on facilitating interventions based on the five principles of Organization Paremiology.

Organizational growth and development are natural processes. They are happening by themselves without intervention all the time. Plants as biological systems have the propensity to grow towards the sun for light and to go deeper into the soil for nutrients. Living systems, including organizations, have the natural propensity to grow bigger and better. The added value that Organization Paremiology brings to the process is 'consciousness – the consciousness to create a more conducive environment for the growth and development to flourish. In achieving better organizational development and growth, consciousness precedes being, which, in turn, precedes doing and relating.

A mistake many organizations make is to seek and initiate Organization Improvement processes when they are already in a crisis. These processes work better when they are done proactively. This gives the organization adequate time to go through the process sanely. They can also go through the process with patience. Life cannot be hurried. We should not wait until when we are very hungry to start seeking help. Prevention is better than cure. If we want a really good and effective Organization Paremiology process, we must be patient. Wisdom does not come overnight. This patience however is not possible in a crisis situation. There are no short cuts to the top of the palm tree.

Stages of the Organization Paremiology process

The success or failure of an Organization Paremiology (OP) process or program is often determined by how well the process is managed. There are five stages in the OP process. These are: the orientation, contracting, organizational assessment, implementation; and monitoring and evaluation phases. Being a long-term process, there are a lot of potential challenges and obstacles along the way.

This chapter will discuss the Organization Paremiology (OP) process and how to manage it effectively. The OP process is about an organization dealing with advice on how to improve its processes. Just as advice is like mushrooms and the wrong type can prove fatal, the type of advice that the organization seeks and uses in the process is of critical importance. Effective management of the OP process is the way for cultivating organizational wisdom.

The orientation phase

It is the sick person who calls for the doctor
The dog that barks the loudest does not bite
Bedbugs are known by the person who sleeps in the room

This phase starts with the organization or its leaders recognizing a need for external support on some issue that needs to be addressed. Only those leaders who have some awareness of what OP is may find it natural to approach an OP practitioner or some other practitioner. Those who do not have such awareness may be at a loss at whom to approach or what to look for in a consultant. It is important that leaders know what to look for in a consultant for their organizational needs to avoid getting wrong mushrooms which may prove fatal to the organization. Impressive qualifications and CVs alone are not sufficient to ensure a consultant will be effective in a situation. Often times, those with the most impressive CVs and qualifications may not be the best thus the proverb, "the dog that barks the loudest does not bite".

In this phase, the client contacts the consultant with a felt need. This might be through a letter, a phone call or a visit. Sometimes it may be through an advert for bidding in a paper. The most important thing is that it must be the client needing the consultant and not vice versa. An OP practitioner can only be effective if he or she is invited and not when he or she invites themselves into the organization. The consultant's power is tied to the invitation.

This phase also involves the first meeting between the consultant and the client to 'understand' the request. Oftentimes what clients ask for may not be what they need. Many times what clients present as their problems may only be symptoms of real and underlying issues. This meeting also helps to know whether OP would be the most appropriate way to address the issue facing the client. After the meeting an agreement is reached whether OP would indeed help in the situation or not. It takes a high level of maturity and professionalism on the side of the consultant to be frank with the client that OP is not what he or she is looking for if this happens to be the case. It is also important to discuss with the client on the 'depth of the intervention that the client is ready for'. Sometimes clients consciously do not want to go deep enough. This too must be respected.

Since there are different approaches that might be employed in improving organizational effectiveness, some of the signs indicating that OP would be more appropriate are:

- The same problem keeps recurring despite various efforts to arrest it;
- You know that there is a problem in the organization but you cannot quite figure out what it is;
- The organization is faced with dilemmas too difficult to resolve;
- The organization is contemplating or has experienced major changes (e.g. change in size, focus, identity, strategy and projects);

- There is confusion about identity, roles and responsibilities;
- There are high levels of staff turnover and frustration;
- There are relationship problems; individuals, departments, board and staff 'do not see eye to eye'; there are high levels of suspicion and lack of trust; people are happier outside the organization than inside;
- Different departments or projects become too autonomous creating co-ordination problems;
- There is a general lack of commitment to the organization and its goals;
- People feel powerless and energy is spent on pointing fingers at each other rather than addressing problems.

After agreeing that the situation would indeed be addressed through OP, the consultant 'listens with two ears' to what the client is asking for and how they feel about what they are asking for. It is important from the onset to gauge the amount of 'energy' in the organization to address what they are asking for. It is important therefore to establish whether it is their problem or somebody else is telling them that they need to address this. In many non-profit organizations, for example, requests that come to the OP consultant are in reality a donor's and not the organization's request. In such situations, the consultant must explain to the client what OP is and what going through an OP process would mean for the client. The consultant must bring home the importance of commitment and ownership to the process on the part of the client, if it is to be a success.

It is also important for the client to concretize the above explanations through sharing with the client his or her experiences. He or she must explain what he or she has observed and learned in working with other organizations in similar situations. The most important thing to explain is that as a process consultant, he or she works with the client and not for the client or to the client. While the consultant will do his or her best, 'working with the client' leaves the responsibility of the success and failure of the OP process with the client.

The contracting phase

Birds agree first before they fly together

Before the actual work starts it is important to formalize the relationship between the consultant and the organization. The contract protects both the organization and the consultant by clarifying what is expected of each party. A contract must specify: expected outputs by the consultant, the role the client will play in supporting the consultant, reporting procedures, how costs will be met; amount of fees to be paid to the consultant and how payment will be made and termination procedures of the contract.

A clarification from these points helps to address some of the potential challenges inherent in the OP process. Some of these challenges are:

Ethical issues – one of the key ethical issues facing many consultants working in situations similar to where we are working is the issue of giving the client 'gifts'. Some clients will 'expect' and sometimes demand the consultant to give them a 'commission' for offering them a contract. This is a very difficult ethical issue in a culture where this is a norm. OP being a profession founded on strong values and ethics, it is important for each consultant to make an ethical stand in their practice and stick with it. We have observed that this issue is relatively more critical among 'beginning' and freelance consultants. Experienced consultants can use their experience and the professional identity they have built during their years of practice to 'frighten off' 'commission seekers'. Consultants operating from an organization can hide behind their 'organizational policies, systems and procedures', which 'do not allow us to do such a thing'. We have found building one's identity through enhancing competence and character to be a main strategy to avoiding being caught up in such unethical behavior. Another way is to have a good hospitality strategy. When clients visit the consultants' organization, it is important to 'treat them well'. This could be through a lunch, a night out or any other legitimate and ethical entertainment. Cultivating an ethical relationship based on mutual respect and trust makes it difficult for the client to demand what he or she may now know is not part of your values and principles. Through such practice, reputation for integrity may spread from actual to potential clients through word of mouth. We have also found 'striving to be the best in the field' or creating a reputation for being the best and therefore making oneself 'indispensable' to be the most effective antidote to having to use or being forced to use bribes.

Some of the unethical issues might include misrepresenting one's qualifications and experience as a consultant, agreeing to undertake an intervention in which one has no skill, experience or competence, colluding with particular groups in the organization to 'attack' the other groups or individuals, forcing the client to go the way the consultant rather than the client wants.

Sustaining interest – many organizations have become accustomed to their chronic problems and they do not care to address them. Many times they will only call for an external consultant because of an acute problem. They will call for a consultant because they are experiencing serious pain. Pain however is only meant to be a motivator for calling for an OP intervention because OP is primarily aimed at addressing the chronic rather than the acute problems. What happens most of the time is that when the pain goes away with the first among the many recommended interventions, the client's interest often wanes. Sustaining the client's interest throughout the process is quite a big challenge. This is why in the contract the client must commit to a long-term process. It may be important to involve the donor sponsoring the process to commit to fund the process rather than a single intervention if need be. Sometimes it may be important to refuse signing the contract if the client only wants to 'use' the consultant on a one-off event as a means to getting funding only as an example.

Belief in foreign consultants – many organizations in developing countries still believe that a consultant must come from America or Europe or at least from outside the country. This is shown through recruitment and remuneration procedures of consultants, which favor consultants from these areas. Where there is an obvious lack of competent local consultants it is justifiable to import consultants from outside. It only becomes an issue when American or European consultants are preferred simply because they are from America or Europe. Competent local consultants have more advantages than imported consultants primarily because they understand their situation better. Combined teams of local and imported consultants may also be appropriate where local and international perspectives are needed. All in all, most organizations have a challenge to overcome the problem of 'too much belief in imported consultants'. At the same time, local consultants need to understand that respect and acceptance are not given on a silver platter, they have to be earned through excellent practice.

Over-dependence on the consultant by the client – As the OP process is progressing, the client may develop more and more dependence on the consultant. The consultant may also want to prolong the relationship more than is necessary for other reasons such as financial gain. Clarification on this matter in the contract helps avoid such situations from arising. This is why the contract must specify the duration of the relationship and clear roles and responsibilities of the client and the consultant. Adherence to these enables the consultant to maintain a healthy social and professional distance from the client. This helps the client to avoid being 'swallowed up' by the culture of the organization. It is important for clients to always remember that the aim of OP is to create increasingly self-reliant organizations, which are more and more capable of solving their own problems and addressing their challenges.

Attention to impact or capacity dilemma – donors' and stakeholders' requirement for organizations to demonstrate impact makes it difficult for the organizations to give enough attention to building their internal capacity. Project activities, writing project and financial reports and deadlines take most of the time leaving none for internal capacity building. Many OP processes are frustrated as 'new projects and activities' suddenly become priorities pushing the OP process into the background. It is important before signing the contract to explain to the client the time demands of the OP process and obtain a commitment that this time will be made available. This must be reflected in the contract.

In order to ensure that the OP process will be a success, it is important at the contracting phase to choose a 'change group' in the organization. This group must be made up of people who can influence others in the organization. It is this group that will be the primary interface between the consultant and the organization during the OP process. The consultant discusses the OP process plan with this group and encourages them to discuss the plan among themselves. The 'change group' is a learning opportunity about leadership and development among the people involved. The consultant is part of this group and he or she eventually withdraws as the OP process is nearing the end. The concept of the 'change group' is a sustainability strategy as it ensures the continuation of the OP process and benefits after the contract with the client has expired.

Organizational assessment phase

A healthy chick comes from a healthy egg

The first activity in the OP program is conducting an assessment. An assessment stems from two main needs.

These are: to know the current health status of the organization and to know the effects of the interventions and take corrective measures as a result.

Assessments must be focused on the whole organization or on the aspect of the organization affected by the issue at hand. Even when the assessment focuses on an aspect of the organization, it is important to undertake it in the perspective of the whole organization. This enables the client to see how efforts in this particular aspect are contributing to overall organizational effectiveness.

To be effective, assessments must be solution rather than problem centered. It is often more effective to ask people what they want first rather than what their problems are. The development model presented in chapter 1 begins with the creation of an ideal picture of the desired situation. The assessment process is therefore based on, "what can help us or hinder us from realizing the ideal picture or the desired situation?"

Data analysis follows data collection. This is usually done in a feedback workshop. Joint data analysis with the client is encouraged for a number of reasons. Among these are: it reinforces ownership of the process, it helps clarify and separate perceptions from real issues and it helps in joint prioritization and action planning.

Part of the data analysis process involves challenging the client to see the contradictions in their behaviors and therefore how their decisions and actions have created the current undesired situation. By seeing how responsible they were in creating the current undesired situation, they are also encouraged to see how responsible they are in creating the desired situation.

To be effective, the assessments must: assess potential for action in the client (readiness, time, resources), help people see the 'whole picture' and the relationships within the picture, focus on the desired future and not to be caught up in the negative past or present and recommend interventions and tasks that people can do for themselves.

For implementation, the plan must show the time frame, the individuals responsible for the activities and indicators that will show whether the activity has been successful or not. This brings us to the next phase, which is:

The implementation phase

It is not by just looking at a newly married wife that she will become pregnant

As stated elsewhere we have observed non-implementation of capacity building plans to be a major challenge in the OP process. The most beautiful and well-constructed capacity building plan will mean nothing if people in the organization do not work to implement it. The commitment of the organization to its own improvement will be known by its commitment to implement the capacity building plan. In order to help the organization implement its capacity building plan and conquer inertia, the following suggestions might help:

Ensure the first intervention is successful – when people are successful the first time, they develop faith to do more in order to create more success. In prioritizing the interventions therefore, it is important to start with those interventions with the highest chance of success. It is also important to start with the easiest and least sensitive interventions. This helps to reduce fear, which is inherent in most change processes. We have observed fear to be a great hindrance among organizational leaders to adopting OP interventions. It is important therefore to be sensitive to this fact.

Give enough authority to the change group – to ensure that the interventions are implemented and followed through, it is important that the leadership in the organization must give adequate authority and responsibility to the change group and not meddle. It then becomes the responsibility of this group to see to it that the capacity building plan is being followed and that the organization is creating the required time and space for the implementation of the capacity building plan. Individual leaders may be 'too busy' to manage the implementation of the capacity building plan. At the same time, giving the responsibility of managing the capacity building plan to the change group offers them a chance to learn and practice leadership skills. In order to ensure that more people benefit, it may be necessary to let people join and leave the change group after some time.

Allocate enough resources to the process – in order to ensure effective implementation, see to it that there are adequate financial and material resources for the process. It is frustrating to get people excited and committed to the process only to end at an anticlimax because there are no resources to continue the process. In our practice, we have observed this to be a major challenge undermining OP programs. At CADECO, we have sometimes waited for two years before an organizational capacity building plan can be implemented because there were no financial resources to back the plan. This is why during the orientation and contracting phase it is important to discuss in detail the financial and material resource implications of the OP process. It may be important to delay starting an OP process and help the organization find adequate resources before engaging in the process. The organization must also be willing to deploy its best people to manage the process. The quality of the people on the change team will determine the success or failure of the process.

Involve all people – in order to be a success, the OP process must gain an organization wide acceptance and commitment. It is therefore important to provide as much information as possible on the aims and activities of the process. It is also important to communicate to the people the successes and achievements of the process, and to celebrate the small successes and achievements. As many people as possible must be involved as much as possible. People will only commit when they feel that they are part and parcel of the change process and that it is in their interest. People will only commit if they are adequately involved.

Do not rush – the time schedules of the capacity building plans must be realistic. It is important to recognize the fact that organizations exist to fulfill their missions by implementing projects in their task environments. They do not exist to build their internal capacity. It is also important to recognize that the success of an organization is not normally measured by how well 'internally capacitated' it is, but by its performance in the task environment. For these reasons, it is important to be realistic with time allocations to the capacity building plans. When we were just beginning our OP practice, we used to cram an organization with OP interventions in a year. We have come to realize that it may take anything between 12 to 24 months and sometimes more to effectively implement an organization's capacity building plan. This gives adequate time to the organization to practice what they have learned in the interventions before going to the next intervention. This strengthens the learning spirit, which is crucial to the success of the OP process.

The Monitoring and Evaluation phase

The person who does not know where he is going will not realize it when he has arrived.
What is the point of running so fast when you are on the wrong road?

Undoubtedly, one of the most challenging issues in managing the OP process is 'how to measure progress. It is relatively easier to measure progress in 'project implementation' as compared to the intangible issues of organizational capacity. It is this lack of clarity on how to measure organizational capacity that sometimes makes it difficult for organizations to convince donors to sponsor their organizational capacity building initiatives. This is because donors want 'hard evidence' that their money is making impact in the organization's task environment.

It is important however to note that an organization's ultimate measure of its capacity is its performance at all levels. These are: efficiency as a measure of activities, effectiveness as a measure of strategies, impact as a measure of goals, legacy as a measure of the mission, and societal transformation as a measure of the vision. The basis of the foregoing reasoning is that only an organization with capacity can produce results in the task environment. One observes that as one moves from efficiency to societal transformation, the organization needs more and more capacity. One also observes that as one moves from efficiency to societal transformation, it becomes more and more difficult to objectively and quantitatively measure progress. It becomes more and more difficult to have clear indicators of progress. This difficulty creates the need for specific indicators of organizational capacity. This makes it possible to measure progress of organizational capacity apart from the results the organization is producing.

Measuring organizational capacity on its own apart from the results the organization is producing makes it possible to show the link between the organization's capacity and its results. This is necessary for organizational leaders and stakeholders to appreciate the importance of organizational capacity building. Through this, it is possible to show that those organizations that have 'more capacity' have also better results in their task environments.

Indicators of organizational capacity are based on the organizational assessment tools used in the organization. Since the assessment measures 'what is the situation?' in the organization, the monitoring and evaluation system measures 'how the situation is changing' using the same assessment factors. The table below illustrates the point:

Table Monitoring and Evaluating an OP process

Rating 0 – 5, 0 = non existent   5 = excellent

Component	Assessment rating	Assessment during or after OP process	Percentage change
1. Financial and material resources			
2. Skills and competencies in the organization			
3. Policies, systems and procedures			
4. Structure			
5. Roles and responsibilities			
6. Strategy			
7. Vision and mission			
8. Culture and values			
9. Governance, leadership and management			
10. External relationships			

The organization must, through consensus or otherwise, rate these components during the assessment phase. After agreeing, the people must give the reasons for the agreed rate. The organization must put in place a monitoring system that will enable it to notice changes on the assessment ratings as the OP process is progressing. At the end of the OP process the organization must also 'measure' the percentage changes from the assessment measures by consensus or otherwise. The people must also give reasons for the new rating. The rates enable the consultant and the client to come up with themes, which point out to the issues needing attention and also an indication over time on how these issues are being resolved.

We have found the above tool to be useful in measuring, objectively and 'quantitatively', the changes resulting from an OP process. Its major weakness however may be that people in the organization may mistake having the 'component' like strategy or a mission statement or policies, which were not there before the OP process, for having built the organization's capacity. The point to emphasize is that it is not having these components that signify capacity, but the benefits that flow from an effective use of these components. For this reason, we have found complementing the above tool with the one below as being more effective in measuring and monitoring organizational capacity.

Table: OP Processes monitoring and Evaluation tool

Rating 0 = extremely poor, 3 = good   5 = exceptionally good

Organizational process	Assessment rating	Rating during or after OD process	Percentage change
1. Strategic leadership			
2. Goal setting			
3. Decision-making, problem-solving and action planning			
4. Effectiveness of communication			
5. Conflict management and resolution			
6. Personal and inter-group relations			
7. Relations between leaders and followers			
8. Individual learning			
9. Team learning			
10. Organizational learning			
11. Use of information and Communication Technology (ICT)			

The above tool is used in the same way as the one above. The strength with this tool is that the processes are much clearer in terms of the benefits they entail, as compared to the components in the first tool. But as stated earlier, it may be more effective to use both tools for complementarity and triangulation.

The assumption in using the above monitoring and evaluation tools is that the organizations and people using them have been oriented to what OP is, and that they understand what the components or processes mean. In other words, they are able to differentiate between when these are 'healthy' or not. Assessing progress using the indicators must be done against the assessment results on one hand, and the 'word picture or ideal picture' on the other.

In some cases, indicators like structure or effectiveness of communication may be too broad. In such cases the people and the organization may need to think of more specific indicators under such categories. The way to go about this is to ask and discuss questions like, "how can we tell if the structure is what we want it to be?" or "how can we tell if the communication is what we want it to be?"

Such indicators therefore may look like:

Structure

- Clarity of organogram among members of staff (0 – 5)
- Clarity of individuals' roles and responsibilities (0 –5)
- Clarity of departmental roles and responsibilities (0 – 5)

Communication

- The level of individual's involvement in project planning (0 – 5)
- Amount of information shared before decisions are implemented (0 – 5)

- Responsiveness of leaders to suggestions from juniors (0 – 5)

The situation may dictate whether to use the headings as indicators or find more refined indicators under the sub-headings. The key however is to enable the organization to consciously move towards its ideal situation as stipulated in the word picture.

Monitoring and evaluation enable the organization to track progress. Monitoring enables the organization to know whether it is still on track regarding its milestones along the way. Evaluations enable the organization to know whether it has achieved its goals or not. Monitoring and evaluations enable the organization to make informed decisions on the way forward.

The most important lessons in managing the OD process

It is not wise to use clutches when one can walk on their own feet

Do not scratch where it does not itch

The most important lesson in the OP process is to seek at every stage to imagine yourself in your client's shoes. This enables the OP practitioner to always genuinely be able to see situations, dynamics and problems from the client's perspectives as well as from your own (Essinger 1994: 123). This discipline of looking at situations from the client's point of view forces the OP practitioner to realize that, "your own priorities and time frames may not be your client's priorities and timeframes" (Essinger 1994: 123).

Related to the above is the need for the OP practitioner to 'assess' the organization's, leading to stage of development and to always be aware of what really matters in general at that particular stage of development. This enables the practitioner to only 'scratch where it is itching'. The use of OP in development organizations for example has been criticized for 'forcing' organizations to 'formalize' before they are readyartificial and mechanical changes. In this situation, it is important to be mindful of the fact that the aim of OP may be helping an organization to make a smooth transition to its next stage of development or to help the organization be the best it can be in its particular stage of development (if it is not 'ripe' to move to its next stage of development). What really matters for organizations that are in the first stage of development, for example, is to ensure positive leadership, manage relationships to ensure team spirit and strengthen transparency and accountability while helping them demonstrate the impact of their work. Scratching where it does not itch may alienate the owners of the organization.

Some lessons on using African proverbs from our practice

We have used African proverbs in OA processes, but also in strategic planning, team building, leadership development, board development and self-development interventions. We have also used African proverbs in working with a range of organizations including: community based organizations (CBOs), professional NGOs, churches and government departments. From this experience, we have learnt a number of lessons, including:

In the proverbs based self-assessment tools, the proverbs act as a 'communication aid or amplifier'. The participants discuss their understanding of the proverbs. They then apply this understanding when answering the question and determining the assessment rate and its explanation (see the example above). We have also learnt that it is often necessary to use an external facilitator to moderate the discussions and the self-assessment process.

It is necessary to use the most fitting proverb to the intervention or situation at hand. Using 'loose' proverbs without a clear link to the intervention or the situation may lead to confusing the people and disrupting the process. The practitioner must always ask himself or herself the question, what is the most effective proverb that I can use in this situation?" In a roles and responsibilities clarification intervention, for example, proverbs like, "if the sun says it is more powerful than the moon, then let it come and shine at night" and the cat in his house has the teeth of a lion" may be very appropriate. In communicating the importance of learning from practice, a proverb like "a person is taller than any mountain they have climbed" would be appropriate.

In training workshops, it is important to use only a few proverbs to maximize their impact. Too many proverbs may lead to loss of interest in the proverbs. This also applies to carrying out assessments using the proverbs based tools. In a three–day team building workshop, for example, we use about three proverbs in one session at the beginning of the workshop to surface issues and insights for discussion. In the proverbs-based assessment tool, this may mean that not all categories may need the proverbs - only where proverbs will add significant value. In other words, proverbs are more useful where a direct question may not surface all the insights because people do not completely understand the question or the issue.

It is important to use reflective questions in order to bring out the insights from the proverbs. Since proverbs may mean different things to different people at different times and in different contexts, the questions must be properly phrased and focused to enable them to solicit only those insights related to the issue at hand. In a self-development session, for example, we use a question like: What insights can we learn from the following proverb: A changed place cannot transform an individual but a transformed individual can change a place. When we used this question and proverb with a rural CBO, a chief explained his total agreement with the proverb by telling the group a story of an individual in his village who migrated to a neighboring country hoping to be 'transformed' by its better economy and somebody else who came from that country to reside in his village. The person who came to reside in his village was a very productive individual and within a short time he became very wealthy. The person who migrated to the other country came back after a few years frustrated and poorer as the 'transformed nation' failed to transform him.

Proverbs can also be used as reflective case studies. To do this more effectively, it is important to know and use the story upon which the proverbs are based. Using a story is especially useful on complicated issues, which are difficult to communicate. For example, it is extremely difficult to teach and communicate organizational identity issues. But using 'proverbs case studies' easily transcends such a barrier. Finally, proverbs must be used naturally and flexibly not mechanically. If used mechanically, the proverbs may actually become a hindrance to the process. The power of proverbs, when used properly, is their 'invisibility' as they serve to facilitate the process rather than draw attention to themselves. This means that proverbs must be used only when their use will add value to the process. Development practitioners must not get too excited with the use of proverbs to the extent of *'using crutches when they can walk on their own feet'*.

Based on the above discussion, helping an organization address its performance issues takes a three tiered model. This model describes an ideal "capacitated' organization developed by the Community Development Resource Association. To do this, the model looks at three key questions:

1. What elements must a "capacitated organization" have?
   i) Vision – the sense of focus and the change the organization wants to bring about in society; ii) Culture – an organization's norms and values, and how these help or hinder the organization; iii) Relationships – how well people in the organization and those within the partnership relate; iv) Strategy – how the organization intends to accomplish its mission; v) Structure – how roles and responsibilities are shared within and among organizations; vi) Policies, systems and procedures – how to bring about consistency in decision-making in

the organization; vii) Skills – whether the organizations have sufficient skill sets or ability to develop these; and viii) Financial and material resources – the adequacy of finances, equipment, and office space, among others.

2. How to balance addressing all the elements for a holistic capacity development effort? It is much easier to address the lower elements (financial and material resources, skills training) than upper elements (vision or culture).

3. What methods are used to ensure effective capacity development service provision? For financial and material resources, providing money is the simplest intervention to develop capacity. Higher element levels involving skills acquisition are addressed by process interventions like facilitation, coaching, mentoring, and reflection and learning.

Concluding remarks

The OP process is basically a learning process built on the proverb, "the world is a school, the earth a classroom and experience, the best teacher." OP interventions and programs are aimed at creating credible, sustainable and high impact organizations. Organizational credibility or integrity, sustainability and impact will result in the following benefits for the people the organizations serve: more physically, mentally and spiritually healthy individuals and communities; more and better job opportunities; more disposable income; and strong and healthy families with children living better lives than their parents. These benefits represent OP's contribution to development and organizational practice.

Undertaking an OP process is the way of cultivating organizational wisdom. It is the way of preparing the organization for the tomorrow it desires, for when one is prepared, difficulties do not come. The use of African proverbs and other forms of indigenous wisdom will play a continually increasing role in the understanding and practice of Organization Paremiology in the unfolding future.

Managing the Organization Development Process

1. What do the following proverbs teach us about when to call for OP interventions and processes?
   To see a snail's eyes one must be patient.
   A fruit does not ripen in a day.
   A patient mouse in a young banana plant will one day eat a ripe banana
   There are no short cuts to the top of the palm tree.

2. How does this proverb describe how conscious we are about our organization's need for external help in the form of consultants?
   It is the sick person who calls for a doctor

3. How does this proverb describe our experiences in working with and what we look for in an external consultant?
   The dog that barks the loudest does not bite

4. What does this proverb teach us about the importance of contracts?
   Birds agree first before they fly together

5. How does this proverb help us see the link between our organizational performance and its internal capacity?
   A healthy chick comes from a healthy egg

6. What does this proverb tell us about implementing capacity building plans?
   It is not just by looking at a newly married wife that she will become pregnant

7. What does this proverb tell us about monitoring and evaluating the implementation of our organization's capacity building plan?

The person who does not know where he is going will not realize it when he has arrived.

CHAPTER EIGHT

Organization Paremiology in Practice: Some Cases

Introduction

Organization Paremiology is practiced at all levels of organization. This is from the personal to the global levels. Being a new field, however, the higher levels are yet to be further developed. In this chapter, I will present three cases as illustrations in the practice of Organization Paremiology.

An Organization level case study on agricultural leadership development

Purpose: to inspire, energize and mobilize innovative leaders, champions, and thinkers in African countries, who are committed to creative new approaches to achieving food security.

Objectives: by the end of the training, participants will be able to:

- Describe their current and potential, formal and informal roles in food security initiatives
- Explore and analyse major challenges in implementing major agricultural initiatives and identify innovative actions that they can take to help overcome these challenges.
- Demonstrate skills necessary for being a champion for change, including such areas as planning, advocacy, and transformative leadership.
- Develop Individual Action Plans to expand their roles and to become active and creative participants in their country and region's ownership of food security initiatives, including outreach to other champions of change and stakeholders.

- Expand their own views of food security and develop advocacy strategies to change mindsets about the role of the very poor, the importance of gender, the role of nutrition in advancing agriculture-led growth, and the impact of climate change on agricultural development.
- Understand their historic roles as part of a Pan-African initiative to tap the most creative thinkers and leaders in finding innovative new ways to meet food security challenges.
- Create sustainable networks to increase agricultural performance and food security.

1. Leadership: African Perspective

Session 1: People centred leadership - Ubuntu
Reflection on the concept of Ubuntu

Session 2: Shadows of African Leadership
Misconception on the African leadership: truths and myths

Session 3: Principles of African Leadership
Reflection on principles of Organization Paremiology

Session 4: Participatory Leadership and Decision Making
Reflection on principles of Ubuntu

2. Responsibility Based Leadership

Session 1: Sowing and Harvesting
Reflections on responsibility based leadership/development

Session 2: Confronting Contradictions
Reflection on the 'the confronting shadows model'

Session 3: Responsibility based approach to Leadership
Practice on responsibility based model and contradictions model

Session 4: Implications for practice of leadership Development

Practice on responsibility based model and contradictions model

3. People and Relationships in Organizations

Session 1: Organizations as extended families
Reflection on the beehive model for team building

Session 2: Importance of team building
Reflection on the story of the elders' council meeting

Session 3: Staff Attraction and Retention
Reflection on the ideal village

Session 4: Organizational Values
Reflection on African values and ethics

4. Conflict Management in Organizations

Session 1: The meaning of conflict
Reflection of African understanding of conflict

Session 2 Levels of conflict in an organization
Reflecting on traditional ways of dealing with conflicts

Session 3: Types of conflict in a community
Reflecting on traditional ways of dealing with conflict in a community

Session 4: Managing conflict in an organization
Application of traditional ways of dealing with conflict in modern organizations

5. Cultivating Leadership And Management Excellence

Session 1: Get Focused
Reflection proverbs and folktales

Session 2: Be courageous
Reflection proverbs and folktales

Session 3: Learn from other people's skills and competencies; do not lose touch with the ground
Reflection proverbs and folktales

Session 4: Do not lose the learning spirit
Reflection proverbs and folktales

6. Knowledge Management

Session 1: The meaning of Knowledge Management
Reflection on traditional knowledge management systems

Session 2: The practice of Knowledge Management
Application of local knowledge management systems in modern organizations

Session 3: Personal Learning and self-development
Reflection on traditional personal development

Session 4: Practice
Application of local self-development in modern self-development

7. Networking

Session 1: The meaning of Networks and Networking
Reflection on the traditional concept of networking

Session2: Types of networks
Application of local understanding of networking in modern organizations

Session 3: Mapping your network
Strengthening networking

Session 4: On line and offline networking
Global positioning through networking building on the traditional understanding

8. Self-Assessments: Self And Organizational Tools
African Proverbs Self-development assessment tool.
African Proverbs Strategic self-assessment tool.

Case 2: A Reflection on values: The Girl and the Sailor

Participants are asked to read the story below. First individually, and then as a group. They are asked to rank the characters from the best to the worst individually and as a group. In coming up with the group ranking it is emphasized that they should arrive at this by consensus, not by voting.

A ship sank in a storm. Five survivors scrambled aboard two life boats: a sailor, a girl, and an old man in one boat; the girl's fiancé and his best friend in the second.

During the storm, the two boats separated. The first boat washed ashore on an island and was wrecked. The girl searched all day in vain for the other boat or any sign of her fiancé.

The next day, the weather cleared, and still she could not locate her fiancé. In the distance she saw another island. Hoping to find her fiancé she begged the sailor to repair the boat and row her to the other island. The sailor agreed, on condition that she sleeps with him that night.

Distraught, she went to the old man for advice. "I cannot tell you what is right or wrong for you," he said. "Look into your heart and follow it." Confused but desperate, she agreed to the sailor's condition. The next morning the sailor fixed the boat and rowed her to the other island. Jumping out of the boat, she ran up the beach into the arms of her fiancé. Then she decided to tell him about the previous night. In a rage, he pushed her away and said, "Get away from me! I don't want to see you again." Weeping she started to walk slowly down the beach.

Seeing her, the best friend went to her, put his arm around her and said, "I can tell that you two have had a fight. I'll try to patch it up, but in the meantime, I'll take care of you".

TASK:

Rank the characters in the story from 1 to 5. 1, being the best character from your point of view and 5 being the worst character. Note down the reasons for your ranking.

Normally the participants will not agree on the ranking and they will have different reasons for their ranking. The Organization Paremiologist uses this to explain the concept of values in organizations, their role and how to make effective use of them.

Cases 3: Organization Paremiology in Community Development Work

In 2008, an international NGO was revising its international programming system. Part of this revision involved a relook of its evaluation and monitoring system. The evaluation and evaluation review involved two aspects. The first was 'international evaluation' and 'local or community based evaluation' and how these two spoke to each other. I was asked to do the local review and develop a new system for local evaluation and monitoring. I did this in Malawi and Swaziland. In this short article I will talk about the method used and how it worked.

2 Methodology

The key issue was the relevance of the development process – bed bugs are known by the people who live in the hut – in other words, the development or evaluation process should be relevant first and foremost to the communities. The international NGO had its own indicators of development but they wanted to be more legitimate, relevant and sustainable. To achieve this, they had to ask some questions. A key question they asked was: what would a good development organization look like to the community? This was in the areas of: a) what would the organization be doing? How would the organization be relating? And how would the organization be in its being? The communities reflected on these three aspects of an organization: the doing, the relating and the being. They came up with their indicators of what a good organization would look like. It is interesting to note that the communities were able to simply define development as 'good change', and based on this, they were able to describe a good organization. They used their description of a 'good' organization to assess the international NGO's effectiveness.

An agreed random sample of communities in six project areas was selected in Malawi and Swaziland. The sample included groups of children, men and women, local government officials, local authorities and local partners. However, the choice sites were also dictated by logistical and time considerations.

The overall approach was consultative and participatory. The methodology employed some techniques of Participatory Rural Appraisal (PRA) – in particular semi-structured interviews, focus group discussions and direct observation. The approaches included:

3. Findings and Discussion

The consolidated findings of all the external stakeholders interviewed are presented in the table below. While sticking to the guiding questions prepared before the actual consultations, the consultant tried to make the questions as open ended as possible in order to let the participants give their 'true indicators or measures without being influenced by the consultant's guidance'. He also intentionally did not give guidance on what 'indicators or measures' should look or sound like, as is conventionally understood, and he did not 'doctor' what the participants presented as their indicators or measures.

Rate 0 – 5, 0 = non-existent, 5 = excellent

Indicator	Rate	Explanation
Activities		
• Meeting the real needs of the people xxx	4,3,4	We identify and design interventions together Generally, people are involved in identification and designing of projects but sometimes projects are imposed to 'get rid' of excess money from WV especially towards the end of some projects or some deadlines. They use an integrated approach to ensure most of our needs are met. In addition, there are visible changes in the lives of the people being served.
• Visible changes in people's lives x	3	There are some changes in people's lives, but there is still some way to go.
• Holistic approach x	4	They include a strong spiritual aspect to their interventions. Many people in the communities are being helped spiritually. But now, we are worried because they have removed the spiritual component budget line.
• Targeting orphans/child focused xx	3,4, 3	WVI is doing commendable work in supporting orphans and poor children, but their help is limited because there are so many such children. There are visible benefits for children. WV encourages other organizations in the area to become more child centered. They pay school fees, give us food, build schools and clothes but not all children who need to be supported are being supported.

• Continuation of benefits after the project has stopped xxx	3, 2, 2	They have told us when the project will come to an end. This forces us to think about how we will continue without them. The committees would help ensure continuity but we still depend on them for the resources.
Relationship with people		
• Democratic xx	4, 4	They always consult with us. They involve us. When we have different priorities we negotiate. They give us the freedom to say no or to tell them we are not ready. They have clear procedures and structures for involving people.
• Works with local leaders xx	4, 4	There are representatives of community leaders in the project management committee. They always consult with leaders on key decisions concerning the communities.
• Follow up support xx	5, 4	'They are always on our heels'. They don't just depend on the reports. They visit to validate the reports. They are committed to follow up. They trust us with community based monitoring and evaluation but they always follow up to validate
Working with other organizations		
• Works in consultation with other organizations xx	4, 3	They work jointly with other organizations. There is no duplication. They also help other smaller organizations in our area We normally work together on issues concerning our expertise and departments/organizations. This

		was poor in the past but it is improving now – (quote from partners).
• Learns from other organizations x	3	We really don't know as we have no way of knowing their internal systems and practices for doing this.
• Planning together xx	3, 4	We don't normally plan together especially annual plans. We usually only plan events together. This is beginning to change for the better though – (quote from partners). There are no duplications of interventions in the area. Being the first organization in the area, they play a coordination role in relation to the new organizations coming into the area – (quote from traditional leaders).
• Sharing resources x	0	This is not happening. Sharing resources could help us achieve more, especially if we decided to implement joint activities – (quote from partners).
Inside the entity		
• Team spirit x	4	They always work together
• Timeliness and keeping time xx	4,4	They try to be timely. Sometimes delays are caused by us, because we are slow to meet some prior requirements. They try as much as possible to stick to promises and agreements.
• Trustworthiness x	4	'We can bank on their words' but sometimes some promises are not fulfilled.
• Fairness/no favouritism xx	3, 2	The criteria for targeting those who need to be helped are clear, but these are usually not followed in practice. There are perceived practices of favouritism in helping children. Some people and children who

		don't need to be helped are being helped while those who need help are not – (quote from children, community members expressed the same sentiment).
• Transparent xx	3, 2	Many things are done transparently but a few, especially those to do with money, may sometimes not be handled as transparently as we would wish – (quote from committee members). They share information with us on new initiatives but they rarely share information on results from those initiatives – (quote from partners)
• Commitment x	4	They are committed to their work. They spend a lot of time with the people they serve.
• Respectful x	4	They listen to us. They always consult us. They are humble. They are practicing Christians. They treat us differently from the other organizations that work with us.

Based on the proverb which says: "bedbugs are known by the people in the hut", the community participants were able to define a good organization, and measured this against the international NGOs. The participants identified performance (under activities), relational (under relationship with us and relationship with other organizations) and organizational indicators (under inside the organization). In comparison with the international evaluation, the indicators or measures identified by the participants are more similar than different. In addition, the international evaluation concentrates on the performance and relational indicators or measures while the participants' assessment concentrates on the organizational indicators or measures as well. It is important to note that the organizational indicators or measures identified by the participants are mostly values they would want to see or they like seeing among the practices of the international NGO.

This aspect was not emphasized in the international evaluation. From the relational indicators, they (especially the partners) would like to see more strengthened partnerships and more resource sharing for synergy. From the organizational indicators, they would like to see more fairness and less perceived favouritism in according opportunities and resources to communities and community members. They would also want to see more transparency especially on money matters.

The use of an Organization Paremiology approach gave the process a more humane approach.

4. Conclusions

The assignment set out to identify evaluation indicators or measures by different external stakeholders, and then to get their rating of the identified indicators or measures and reasons behind the rates. The stakeholders were community members, committee members, children, traditional leaders and representatives of partner organizations. They identified their own performance, relational and organizational measures or indicators. Using the same, they also assessed the capabilities of the international NGO. It was observed that the identified measures were generally congruent with measures in the international evaluation. The only exceptions were the organizational measures or indicators. To ensure alignment, it may be necessary to include this category in the international evaluation.

It was observed also that the external stakeholders generally perceive the international NGO to be a good organization. From the performance indicators, however, they are concerned about the 'continuity of the project benefits after the international NGO leaves the community'. From the relational indicators, they (especially the partners) would like to see more strengthened partnerships and more resource sharing for synergy. From the organizational indicators, they would like to see more fairness and less perceived favouritism in according opportunities and resources to communities and community members. They would also want to see more transparency especially on money matters.

Case 3: Organization Paremiology in Reflection at the National level

Why do people smear themselves with mud and then complain that they are dirty?

Recently, I found myself at breakfast at Nkopola Lodge in Malawi with a colleague from the world of international NGOs. Since both of us had spent most of our adult lives as development workers in Southern Africa—he is Norwegian and I am from Malawi—we started comparing the different experiences of the countries that we've worked in, especially Norway and Zambia, where we have spent the most time and energy.

For Zambia at Independence in 1964, copper was the driving force of the economy, making it the second-richest country in Africa at the time (South Africa was the first). During the same period, Norway was a relative backwater in Europe. But today, Zambia is one of the poorest countries in the world, and most Zambians are significantly poorer than they were at Independence. Meanwhile, Norway is one of the richest—in fact it is the second best country on the planet for a child to be born in terms of future quality of life (Switzerland is just ahead).

> My colleague's explanation for these different trajectories was that Zambia's copper enriched North Americans and Europeans in the same way that it is enriching Chinese companies today, always at the expense of the Zambian people. Revenue from copper was used to subsidise consumption rather than to invest in building a strong and sustainable economy. The continued weakness of countries like Zambia works to the advantage of foreign investors, because it offers them the opportunity to externalize Africa's resources with considerable ease.

By contrast, Norway discovered oil in the North Sea in the late 1960s, and used the resulting revenue to build a national endowment, now part of an even larger Government Pension Fund. If the money in the Fund were to be distributed among the Norwegian population, each person would get at least $150,000 in cash. However, my friend was quick to point out that this would not be necessary, because the Norwegian Government functions pretty well in meeting its obligations towards its citizens.

The real difference between Zambia and Norway, we both agreed, is not one of resources but one of leadership, management and governance: while Norway is busy building its future, Zambia is busy 'smearing itself with mud and complaining that it is dirty', to quote the words of an old African proverb from Kenya. Corruption remains rife, with the 2015 Anti-Corruption Act widely ignored by the police and the judiciary, in public services and land administration. And there is little by way of a political consensus or constituency to prioritize long-term social and economic goals.

In other words, Zambians still have not taken their destiny into their own hands by establishing a vision for the future, a system of governance to put it into practice, and a leadership culture that is prepared to set aside parochial concerns. So what has to be done?

At the time of my breakfast conversation at Nkopola Lodge I had just turned 40, and I was increasingly frustrated by the condition of the aid industry in Africa and its failure to engage with the long-term transformation of the continent. Colin Grant's biography of Marcus Garvey, A Negro with a Hat, was one of my favourite inspirations, written in 1914 and urging Africans to rise up and forge their own future by "dash[ing] asunder the petty prejudices within your own fold… be Negro in the light of the Pharaoh of Egypt, Simon of Cyrene, Hannibal of Carthage…who have made and are making history for the race though deprecated and in many cases unwritten."

Yet today, a full century later, what has really changed? Some say that a significant shift has already taken place on the continent, with greater self-confidence and rising rates of economic growth. But inequality and corruption are still rising, so perhaps the major shift has been in the identity of the oppressors. First they were outsiders in the form of slave traders and colonialists, while today they are insiders too—aid workers, politicians, bankers, industrialists and the odd NGO or two.

African heads of state will blame lack of resources or inadequate funding from the rich world as the cause of all the problems facing their societies. But poor governance and lousy leadership are ultimately the responsibility of Africans themselves. Self-oppression is perhaps the most damaging of all, and if we're ever going to get ourselves out of this mess, then we have to look deep inside to uncover and address the history and psychology of the forces that have brought Africa to this point.

My contribution to that process has been to recover African proverbs, folktales and traditions as a way of illuminating the dilemmas of governance and leadership today. Just in case the development industry lacked sufficient jargon, it is now been codified into a formal field called "Organization Paremiology"— the use of indigenous wisdom in proverbs to improve the performance of institutions. This is especially important given that most organizational development advice and training in Africa is inspired by experience and research in Western Europe and North America.

Proverbs are an integral part of African culture. They are simple statements with deep meaning that serve as guidelines for individual and collective behaviour, having been built on repeated real life experiences and observation over time. By using African proverbs, Organization Paremiology simplifies and clarifies complex subjects and opens up new avenues for action, capturing the essence of a problem in language that is easy to understand and internalise –as when a country 'smears itself with mud and complains that it is dirty.'

For example, *"If the sun says it is more powerful than the moon, then let it come and shine at night."* I've used that proverb many times to uncover hidden debates about hierarchy and power, and how roles and responsibilities develop inside organizations. Or take this one: *"The river that forgets its source will soon dry up,"* a great way of talking about the primacy of values in any system or institution. One good proverb can capture in a sentence what a classic organizational development book would need a whole chapter to accomplish.

To be fair, I have not yet used this approach in national-level discussions about politics and governance, but there is no reason why it could not be just as useful in that context—for example, in debating how Zambia could improve the governance of its natural resources, or changing how decisions are made about who benefits from their extraction. A good starting point would be to re-negotiate existing deals with Chinese companies to reduce the externalization of resources, build tax revenues, and encourage investment in the local economy. That would help to ensure that the Zambian state has the resources it needs to work for its citizens.

Confidence in the political process could be strengthened using deliberative platforms (real and virtual) that enable people to discuss their concerns and hold their representatives accountable for their actions. Decentralization policies that are already on the books could actually be implemented as a first step in re-orienting the benefits of Zambia's skewed economy to rural areas. And a 'right of recall' could be established to deal with leaders who are absent from their constituencies for long periods of time (a common problem in the country).

When citizens are able to undertake these kinds of actions, they will begin to address their own self–oppression and be better positioned to help in creating systems of governance, leadership and accountability that can drive the continent forward. Let's 'take a proper bath and stop complaining that we are dirty.'

Conclusions

As illustrated above, Organization Paremiology will play a key role in the development and business discourse and narrative in Africa and indeed the world. This will be at all levels from individual to global. Organization Paremiology will be able to put issues in a language that Africans understand better. Organization Paremiology will also position Africa better at a global level with an original and authentic contribution. Being a new field, there is need for more and better examples from practice at all levels.

CHAPTER NINE

The Organization Paremiologist

Organizational leaders and Organization Paremiologists work together in cultivating organizational effectiveness. While the primary role of organizational leaders is to find solutions to their organizations' challenges and demands, the primary role of the organization paremiologist is to help the leaders better understand the challenges and demands so that they can find more effective solutions. This chapter discusses some lessons for Organization Paremiologists and provides insight for improving their effectiveness as change agents.

Role of the Organizational Paremiologist

The process by which an organization matures through the dependent, independent and interdependent stages is a natural one and can happen in a number of ways. The role of the Organization Paremiologist as a change agent is to facilitate and add more consciousness to the process. One of the ways is through the Organization Paremiology approach. Organization Paremiology is a holistic approach to improving an organization's impact, sustainability and integrity aimed at creating and nurturing an empowering organizational culture as a basis for organizational improvement efforts (Malunga, 2013).

Some of the signs that an organization needs an Organization Paremiology intervention include:

- The same problem keeps recurring despite serious efforts to arrest it
- There is a problem in the organization but no one can figure out what exactly it is

- The organization is faced with dilemmas too difficult to resolve
- The organization is contemplating or has experienced a major change (e.g change in size, focus, identity, strategy, and /or projects)
- There is confusion about identity/roles and responsibilities
- There is a high level of staff turnover and frustrations
- There are relationship problems among individuals and in departments, and the board and staff disagree. The high level of suspicion and lack of trust cause people to be happier outside the organization than inside
- Departments or projects become too autonomous creating coordination problems
- There is a general lack of commitment to the organization and its goals
- People feel powerless and energy is spent pointing fingers at each other rather than addressing the problems

In short, the Organization Paremiology process is appropriate for organizations that are:

- In a crisis
- Doing well but facing a crisis in the short run
- Doing well but wishing to build on their strengths for more success

In working with the client organization, organizational consultants play different roles as the situation demands. Each situation is unique, requiring a unique response. The main roles organizational consultants can play are:

Supporter - The consultants give the client organization a sense of worth, value, acceptance, and support in its development efforts.

Raiser of consciousness - The consultant helps the client organization generate data and information in order to restructure perceptions. The consultant acts as a mirror of reality of the situation and how things could be.

Confronter - The consultant points to value discrepancies in the beliefs and actions of those working in and with the organization.

Prescriber - On rare occasions, it becomes necessary to tell the client organization what to do to solve the problem.

Trainer - The consultant teaches the client organization concepts, frameworks, and principles so that the client organization can diagnose and solve its own problems.

MAJOR TYPES OF OD INTERVENTION	
DIAGNOSIS	To ascertain problems. The traditional data-collection and fact-finding methods are commonly used, including interviews and questionnaires.
TEAM BUILDING	To enhance the effective operation of systems
INTER-GROUP	To improve the effectiveness of independent groups. The focus is on joint ventures.
SURVEY FEEDBACK	To analyse the data produced by a survey and design appropriate action plans based on collected data.
EDUCATION AND TRAINING	To improve skills, abilities and knowledge of individuals in areas such as leadership and governance development and financial management.
RESTRUCTURING	To improve the effectiveness of the technical or structural aspects affecting individuals or groups. Examples include job enrichment, matrix structures and management objectives.
GRID ORGANIZATION DEVELOPMENT	To use a six-phase change model involving the entire organization.
THIRD-PARTY PEACE MAKING	To manage conflict between two parties.
COACHING AND COUNCELLING	To better enable individuals to define learning goals, reflect on how others see their behaviour, explore alternative behaviours and learn new ones.
LIFE AND CAREER PLANNING	To help individuals identify life and career objectives, capabilities, strengths and deficiencies and strategies for achieving objectives.
PLANNING AND GOAL SETTING	To include theory and experience in planning and goal setting. May be conducted at individual, group or organizational levels.
STRATEGIC MANAGEMENT	To help key policy makers identify their organization's basic mission and goals; ascertain environmental demands, threats and opportunities; and engage in long-term action planning

OD consultants can perform these roles in a variety of different types of interventions. These interventions correspond roughly to the types of challenges that an organization may be facing, from weak leadership or interpersonal conflict to restructuring and strategic planning. These interventions can be grouped into 3 types. By understanding which type of OD intervention he or she is working on, an OD consultant will be able to focus his or her energy, as well as the energy of the staff of the organization.

Lessons for consultants

The following are some of the lessons consultants can use to improve their effectiveness.

Need for personal transformation

A changed place cannot transform an individual but a transformed individual can change a place.

Intervening in the lives of other people and organizations is an enormous responsibility with serious implications for the consultant. The essence of organizational change lies in interventions of transformation to bring about sustainable change in the individual or the organization. It is a simple human principle that people cannot give what they do not have. Consultants cannot bring about individual, team, and organizational transformation if they are not transformed themselves.

Good consultants are alive and awake all the time. They involve their whole being in each undertaking. They stay in touch with their purpose and use their skills, experiences, emotions and position rather than being used by them. They go with the flow but are not afraid to go against the majority. They live in different worlds without being swallowed by any. They see dilemmas as opportunities for creativity. They see the environment through the eyes of purpose. Therefore, in order to be effective, organizational practitioners must not neglect their own self-development.

Another aspect of the above proverb on transformation points toward the need for people in the organization to change for the organization itself to change. The work of organizational consultants must ultimately be directed at transforming people and not merely things. Even the best structures, strategies and systems sooner or later reflect the hearty of the people in the organization. On the other hand, transformed people clearly see the need to change and improve even the worst structure, strategy and systems.

While changing things and people usually go together, focusing on transforming people is more important because this is where the sustainability of change lies. Transformed people can change things themselves and because of this, they will own and sustain the change.

Marketing consultancy services

Good merchandise sells itself, if someone offers to cover you in cloth you should first see what clothes they are wearing themselves.

Organizational improvement practice in NGOs, especially in Africa and other developing regions, is still new. As such, awareness of it is also low. The concept of capacity building among many NGOs remains limited to the acquisition of material resources and training. The full benefits of process interventions are still not known. For this reason, it is important for organizational consultants to think through how they will market their services.

One of the major lessons we have learned from CADECO's practice is that aggressive methods do not work when it comes to selling organizational improvement services. As long as people do not feel any pain in their organizations, they see no need for calling for a consultant. In fact, leaders are often reluctant to call in consultants because they cannot differentiate between what situations can be better handled within the organization and what situations call for external consultants.

Organizational leaders will often call for consultants only when they:

- Have been told by donors to carry out an evaluation or baseline survey and they dare not disobey their donors;
- Have a deep problem threatening their survival or that of their organization.

In other words, leaders generally call organizational improvement consultants only in limited situations. The long-term nature of process interventions explains why few go through a complete organizational change program. Once the pain that motivated them to call for help goes away after the first or second intervention, they discontinue the process to the detriment of the organization.

The marketing implications of this are that, like a medical doctor, the consultant cannot force an organization that feels pain to come to the clinic. Directly soliciting work backfires in most instances since the wrong signals are sent to the potential client, and this reduces the power of the consultant.

A more effective way of marketing organizational improvement services is to make one's services and one's self more attractive to potential clients. More effective ways of marketing organizational improvement services involve bringing awareness of process consulting, benefits, and how it works to potential clients. If possible, give concrete examples of similar organizations that have greatly benefited from similar services. The aim is to make potential clients:

- Know you and the uniqueness of your services.
- Trust you, your knowledge and experience: 'show the clothes you are wearing'.
- Prefer you to your competitors.
- Choose you rather than your competitors

Overall, the strongest marketing strategy for the organizational consultant is to provide high quality service.

Listening to everyone

Taking action based on one person's view is provoking wasps in a nest.

Consultants must be conscious of special dynamics. Often clients will come to the consultant with a predetermined problem and preconceived solution framed from the point of a small number of people in the organization, usually the leaders. For example, a client may come and ask the consultant to help stop the problem of high staff turnover. In order to truly help, the consultant must not rush to prescribe solutions before fully understanding the problem and its underlying causes. He or she needs to listen to objectives and to all parties in the organization.

It is important to maintain the attitude that everyone has something worthwhile to say no matter who they are. There is always a danger of the consultant being swayed away by more persuasive individuals in the organization and ending up siding with one particular group only to earn resentment from the other. Because some people are not able to speak freely in workshops or group settings, it is important to carry out anonymous individual interviews so that those people can freely speak their mind.

Since the leaders often frame problems, it is important to prepare them for any surprise that may come from the interviews. Often those in leadership see things differently than the staff does, which often causes the problem. Leaders tend to disassociate themselves from problems because they are the ones asking for the consultants help and often work closely with him or her. This gives them the impression that they are part of the solution rather than the problem and that the problem lies with other members of the organization. On the other hand, other members might think that the leader is the problem and removing him or her would do away with all the problems.

Seeing beyond words

To see a snail's eyes, one must be very patient
To the man who has a hammer in his toolkit, every problem looks like a nail

Each person and organization has a shadow that they try to protect. We all tend to think that we are good people and that there is a problem with the other person. When talking to people therefore consultants may not be able to get the full picture of the problem from words alone. A full range of skills and tools is critical for the consultant to be able to effectively address the whole range of the organizational issues encountered. In particular, the Organization Paremiologist must develop skills to see beyond the words and see hints in ways people interact, the way offices are arranged, the artefacts in the buildings such as wall hangings, the way resources are allocated and utilized, etc. He must be able to observe these and bring out contradictions to the consciousness of the individuals and groups concerned. This is a critical skill for helping organizations to move beyond their stuck points.

For the organizational paremiologist, seeing what the leaders of the organization are not seeing is a key skill in helping organizations move from their stuck places. This sometimes demands a great deal of patience, but ultimately, people can only transform when confronted with contradiction of what they say and what they truly are.

The quality of questions

It is the hand that tied the lion that knows best how to untie it

The key difference between Organization Paremiology and other consultancies is that Organization Paremiologists bring questions to the organization rather than providing solutions.

The basic belief in Organization Paremiology is that solutions people create themselves are more relevant and long lasting than those coming from the consultant. The way to create these solutions is through working with developmental questions. Solutions are situation specific. What worked in one organization may not work in another organization. No one knows their situation better than the leaders of the organization do. Developmental questions are the means to surface situation specific solutions. While providing guidance, the Organization Paremiologist asks questions that help staff to:

- Focus on issues at hand
- Observe trends, patterns, and events that will help explain the issue
- Dig deep to understand the underlying causes of the problem
- State what they want to see changed in the situation
- Evaluate alternative actions to be taken, based on their consequences
- Analyse obstacles to be overcome
- Identity what can be done from within the system and what external support is needed
- Decide upon the best action and how it will be taken

The answers to all these questions can only be found within the organization because, at some level, those inside the organizations know best how the organization operates and what is needed to strengthen it. The Organization Paremiologist only encourages the organization to open its own bag of solutions.

Organization Paremiology success greatly depends on the ability of the Organization Paremiologist to ask the questions the client would ask. The questions must express his or her understanding and interpretation of the clients own, and real questions concerning the situation or issue at hand. The

Organization Paremiologist also must support the client to live with the questions without rushing to immediate answers. The more the client holds the question, the more it grows and the more it awakens consciousness within the client system. It is important, therefore, that the Organization Paremiologist listens deeply so that he or she can express the real question (s) of the client and not his or her own. While the Organization Paremiologist may find the words, he or she must always ensure that the question and eventually the answer come from from the client.

Interviewing into Organizational culture

A guest sees more in an hour than a host sees in a year

A finger does not point at its owner

Culture has a tendency to sedate all that comes into it. Remaining conscious takes effort. The influence of culture takes over so gradually that it is usually unnoticed. New people see so much in a new setting that gradually fades with increased exposure.

The greatest leverage of the Organization Paremiologist is that he or she is an outsider to the client system and is able to see much more than the people inside the organization. Organization Paremiologists must always maintain newness and avoid being swallowed up by the culture of the organization. Consultants who have been absorbed by the culture of the organization stop being objective and effective.

Working in an organization as an Organization Paremiologist for a long period of time can be dangerous. It is better to work for shorter periods of time with breaks, rather than establishing a permanent office in the client organization. This is a particular challenge for organizations' internal consultants.

Another advantage Organization Paremiologists have is to be able to 'speak the unspeakable' because they are not caught up in organizational politics. People in the organization often do not give each other adequate feedback for fear of destroying relationships. The proverb about the finger is particularly true in this respect as staff members are usually reluctant to implicate themselves or other close colleagues to avoid contributing to problems within the organization. But sometimes, admitting to being part of the problem may help.

Intervening into power and organizational politics

One cannot tell who is going to lose until the fight is over

While coming from a walk with his children, the little frog was confronted by a francolin and they started to fight. Terrified by the gigantic size of the francolin compared to their father, the frog's children ran home and told everyone that their father had been killed. When friends and family members went to see the sight of the fight, they were surprised to see the frog alive and the gigantic francolin dead. While the francolin was physically stronger the frog had a poisonous skin that killed the opponent. The moral of the story is: do not judge who will win or lose before the fight is over.

When Organization Paremiologists go into an organization, they must be aware that they are intervening in a political system where different types of power interplay. They must be able to identify the power points and how these affect organizational effectiveness. The picture of power on the surface may not be the real one in practice. There are organizations where the secretary is more powerful than the director for example.

Power is connected to decision making. In the wrong hands, power leads to negative politics. Powerless people cannot make big decisions. The role of the Organization Paremiologist is to help the organization establish positive politics. This is one of the most complex roles for an Organization Paremiologist and requires a lot of his or her maturity.

The Organization Paremiologist must analyse the power points, identify the positive and negative elements, and then intervene to strengthen the positive elements and defuse the negative ones.

No one wants to be stripped of power and individuals naturally resist any efforts perceived as doing so. Organization Paremiologists must know how to deal with resistance in individuals, groups and organizations. Power dynamics often become clear in conflict management and resolution interventions. Power translates into the ability to do work. Therefore, identify people with power, either positive or negative and work with and through them to be effective.

Coaching and accompaniment

What elders see while sitting, the young cannot see while standing on their toes.

No matter how sharp a knife is, it cannot cut itself

Organization Paremiologists must be realistic about their capabilities and be able to measure their capacity against the interventions they are being asked to undertake. It it important to recognize one's limitations and work with rather than against them. Organization Paremiologists must climb trees that are too tall for them. Frequently, young and inexperienced consultants agree to undertake big and complex assignments only to do more than good to both the organization and themselves.

It is important for younger and less experienced Organization Paremiologists to have mentors and coaches to support them.

When faced with a new intervention, it is important to work under a more experienced Organization Paremiologist and learn from him or her. Organization Paremiologists also need a speaking partner. These are individuals with whom they regularly exchange ideas and gain different perspectives. An example of the importance of being humble and patient to work with a good mentor is given below.

Two men come to a river and look for a place to cross. The current is very strong and they are both afraid to cross it. A third man comes along and sees their difficulty. He leads them up the river to a place where there are some stepping-stones and a small island in the middle of the river. He urges the men to step on the stones but both are afraid, so he agrees to take one of them on his back. By the time he gets to the middle of the river, the man on his back seems very heavy, so he puts him on the little island. He then returns to fetch the second man who wants to climb on his back as well. But the third man refuses. Instead he takes his hand and encourages him to use the stepping stones himself. Halfway across, the second man starts to manage alone and drops the third man's hand. They both cross the river. When the two of them get to the other side, they are extremely pleased with themselves and they walk off together, completely forgetting about the first man, sitting alone on the island. He tries to get their attention, but they do not notice his gestures for help.

Empathizing with the client

The sympathiser cannot mourn more than the bereaved

Organization Paremiologists must remember that the problems are those of the client organization and not their own. The organization paremiologist's role is to help the client not to carry their problems for them. Many times people tend to throw their problems on the consultant. He or she can empathize, but taking the problems as his own or her own is wrong. Indeed, if Organization Paremiologists took the clients problems on their shoulders, the amount of stress would be indescribable. Organization Paremiologists must have faith that people have the capacity to deal with their own problems. His or her role is to provide the information, knowledge alternatives necessary to make informed decisions. The Organization Paremiologist has no power to change an organization; only people in the organization can do that.

When faced with a desperate organizational situation, the temptation is high to become too sympathetic and the line between sympathy and empathy becomes blurred, leaving the consultant open to losing objectivity. Lasting solutions to the problems in organizations are the ones that people create for themselves. It is difficult to facilitate the process when the Organization Paremiologist is too sympathetic and encourages dependence, taking away the client's sense of opportunity.

Ensuring ownership of interventions

You can take the goat to the river, but you cannot force it to drink

Three issues are critical for an Organization Paremiologist to consider before starting an intervention. These are readiness, time and other resources allocated. The leadership of the organization must be genuinely committed. The staff must take more ownership than the organizational paremiologist. The time needed for the Organization Paremiology process must be agreed upon in advance. This is normally anything from six months to two years. It is also to agree and commit to the overall resources needed for the process, including staff time, meetings and workshops.

The true success of an Organization Paremiology process is its implementation after the consultant has left, implying that change has taken place within the organization's culture. When an intervention is over and the Organization Paremiologist is gone, the staff have to decide whether they will implement the strategic plan formulated, whether they will sustain the team spirit developed in the team building workshop. Only staff can decide to use the new policies, systems and procedures developed. The Organization Paremiologist may influence, but has no power on these decisions. When people do accept changes affecting organizational culture, they will sustain them long after the Organization Paremiologist is gone

CHAPTER TEN

The Organization of Tomorrow

Introduction

An effective organization is based on the principles of Organization Paremiology. Ubuntu intentionally practices human values of building community all the time. In short, an effective organization is Ubuntu in action in an organization with the aim of sustaining healthy relationships and empowering the people to maximize their potential.

Creating and nurturing the organization of tomorrow

The presentation that follows is built from Organization Paremiology practice by the author over the last 20 years. It draws on the work of Edgar Schein (2010), Peter Senge (1990); and Senge and others (2008). It shows that the future organization will no be 'African' but global, standing on the African heritage. The practice of Organization Paremiology emphasises the concepts of Ubuntu to Organizational Learning and Culture.

Proactivity

Sustaining healthy relationships and getting inspiration are not ends in themselves. The aim is to create increasing capacity for problem solving in the organization. A conducive environment in the organization creates a healthy environment for creativity to solve problems and innovation. The effective organization focuses on its circles of control and influence and believes that in these circles no problem is insolvable. In an African community, this is the work of leadership personified by the council of elders. The elders meet regularly to discuss issues facing the community. A specific role of the elderly members of the council is to remind the young ones of what they have learnt about life and which may be of relevance today. Organization Paremiology plays a key role in this.

Commitment to learning to learn

Many organizations do not understand the meaning of organizational learning. Most organizations mix up organizational learning with work review. What is called organizational learning in these organizations is actually work review. People meet to discuss and plan work objectives.

In a proper learning session, people come to discuss the environment in the organization. In a spiritual organization, the people go beyond this to discuss:

- How do we understand and apply the concepts of love and Ubuntu in this organization?
- How do these affect our work relationships and work results?

Proverbs and folktales are theorems for understanding key issues of life. Learning from proverbs and folktales is much richer and deeper and more meaningful.

Monkey and goat

Once upon a time the goat and the monkey were very good friends. One day, the Goat asked the monkey how he managed to look so strong, healthy, happy and well-fed throughout the year while for him, Goat, he was well-fed only during the rainy season when grass was plentiful, while he starved and struggled for the rest of the year. "Ah for that you need to learn how to get food from different sources throughout the year", the Monkey replied. "To master the diversification of your food sources, you need to learn some six lessons and after that you will never struggle again", the Monkey continued. "When can we start?" The Goat asked, excitedly.

They met the next day for the first lesson. "Lesson number one is called, when the grass is finished on the ground, go for the low hanging fruits and leaves in trees," the Monkey said. He demonstrated to the goat on how to stand on two feet and put the front legs on the trunk of the tree and nibble away the low hanging leaves and fruits. He then asked the Goat to try. Goat tried and in no time he was eating the leaves and fruits successfully. "Time up, it's time to go to lesson number two", the Monkey shouted. "No, Monkey, I am OK with lesson number one. I am happy with the low hanging fruits and leaves", the Goat replied and kept on eating. "There are five more lessons, remember," the Monkey said. "Yes, I remember but lesson number one is enough for me, I am happy. Leave me alone", the Goat replied. The Monkey tried to persuade the Goat but to no avail.

Confused and disappointed, the Monkey left the Goat alone while the Goat looked happy and satisfied.

Positive assumptions about human nature (Theory Y)

Organization Paremiology aims at building the positive side of people. By surfacing and confronting contradictions, it shows that people are generally good. All people want good things for themselves and others. The effective organization builds on this positive side of people. Effective people are not perfect. But they are conscious of their 'shadows' or 'contradictions'. And they confront them. A key agenda item of an effective organization is to reflect on and minimise its shadows and contradictions.

Belief that the Environment can be Managed

Organization Paremiology believes that with unity – the most formidable challenges in the task environment can be resolved – Unity among cattle makes the lion lie down hungry. Organizations are established to solve problems in the task environment. If there were no problems in the task environment the organization would not exist. Through effective collective reflection on the organization's uniqueness, the organization creates leverage in managing its environment. An effective organization believes in the power of thought and insight to rise to the point of challenges offered by the environment all the time (King, 1969:44). The power of belief backed with appropriate action is what distinguishes a spiritual organization.

Mr. Banda lived in a thug-infested area in Nairobi. His house got broken into a number of times. "Get a good dog" a friend advised him. Mr. Banda went to town and bought what he was told was a good dog.

After one week, his house got broken into again. Mr. Banda went back to the dog seller. The seller said the dog he bought could not bite and could not bark even though it looked fierce. He would do better by buying another one that would bite the thieves when they came again.

Mr. Banda bought another dog – this time, one that could bite. After one week, his house got broken into again. He was frustrated again and went back to the dog shop.

"Oh, I forgot to tell you. This one you bought for the second time can bite, but it can't bark because it does not have good eyesight to see the thieves", the dog seller said.

"What should I do", Mr. Banda asked. "Oh buy another one with good sight and a strong bark," the dog seller advised.

Mr. Banda bought the third dog. With the three dogs no thief ever came to his house again.

Commitment to Truth through Pragmatism and Inquiry

When the council of elders meet, one of the key agenda is to give each other honest feedback regarding conduct and performance. Many organizations are afraid to know the truth about themselves. They overrate their strengths and under-rate their weaknesses. Spiritual organizations are committed to truth. People in the organization give each other honest feedback. They do regular organizational reviews and they are not defensive when the results of such reviews show that the organization is not doing well. The organization as a whole listens to feedback both from within and without the organization and acts accordingly.

Positive orientation towards the future

Organization Paremiology believes that every proverb is a sacred text, that proverbs reflect the divine, and that life itself is a proverb of creation. And indeed, Organization Paremiology asks, "what is not sacred?" It is upon this that the future orientation of Organization Paremiology is based.

The people in an effective organization believe that they are an instrument of the Spirit. They also believe that their mission is of the Spirit. They believe that as long as their mission is relevant and they are taking the rightful activities to implement the mission, the Spirit will continue to sustain and empower them. They also believe that their work is contributing to a better future for mankind on earth.

Commitment to Full and Open Task – relevant communication

Organization Paremiology believes that a repeated incision shines brighter – in other words, free flow of communication is a key distinguishing feature of a spiritual organization. Where there is dialogue and agreement, there is God.

Each person has access to all the information they need to do their work well. A spiritual organization invests heavily in effective knowledge management. They are able to differentiate between useful and not so useful information and knowledge. Spirituality being a new field in most organizations, the leaders make available as much information as possible to the people on this issue. Even more importantly, the organization develops its own knowledge through reflection and learning on Ubuntu.

Commitment to cultural diversity

Knowledge is like a baobab tree, no one person can embrace it alone

The effective organization takes as many lenses as possible for looking at an issue. This helps to accommodate people from different cultures and backgrounds. It also helps in formulating a synergistic understanding of issues. This involves reflecting, with different groups, on such questions as:

Where we come from:

- What does the concept Ubuntu mean?
- How similar or different is it when we see what is practised in this organization?
- Which elements from our background can we adopt? Which elements should we drop and which elements can we modify?
- How can we create synergy from our different backgrounds?

Commitment to systemic thinking

An effective organization looks at the whole and not only parts of the organization. It thinks about interconnectedness – judge each day not by its harvest, but by the seeds you sow unto it. The conceptualization of the organization is one of an organism not a machine. People in an effective organization are encouraged to think about their organization in this way and to see each individual or department as important.

In a village, Mr. Phiri is riding his bicycle to a faraway village. Along the road, he finds Mr. Ssempebwa stuck with his bicycle. Mr. Ssempebwa has a punctured tyre. "Excuse me sir, may you please help me with your pump so that I can fix my punctured tyre?" Mr. Ssempebwa asks Mr. Phiri.

"I am in a hurry, and why did you not pick your own pump when starting your journey?", Mr. Phiri answered while proceeding with this journey.

After about two hours while still cycling home, the weather suddenly changed and it began to pour very heavily. Mr. Phiri could not proceed with his journey. He asked for shelter at the nearest house he could find.

A happy woman welcomed him together with her children. They asked him to wait in their seating room. They prepared a hot drink for him. He was comfortable and happy.

As the rain was coming to an end, he heard a knock on the door and in came Mr. Ssempebwa. "We had this gentleman here with us; he was taking shelter from the rain." Mrs. Ssempebwa said excitedly. "Oh this one, I already met him on the road" Mr. Ssempebwa said nothing more.

After finishing his drink, Mr. Phiri quickly said good bye and left. After two days he came back with a goat to apologise. Mr. Phiri and Mr. Ssempebwa became good friends.

Patience

What do we mean when we talk about applying an effective Organization Paremiology focus to organizations? Assume that you have some influence in your organization. How would you go about creating an organization (or a department) that is using an Organization Paremiology focus?

The quick answer is, "very carefully." There is no formula. You decide where you want to go and go there. The piece that is usually missing in most organizations is that people don't really decide where they want to go.

Patience in creating an effective organization

Once upon a time in a village, there was a couple that loved each other so much. But this couple had a problem. They had no child. They tried all they could to have a child to no avail. They then resorted to prayer.

By a miracle, the woman became pregnant and and gave birth to a handsome baby boy. The boy was named Talandira because he was born late, 15 years after their wedding.

The boy grew up and was very active playing with friends. One day, Talandira was playing with his friends, and they were chasing one another in trees. Unfortunately, he missed a branch and fell to the ground. He had so much pain in the leg. His parents took him to the hospital. The doctors said that he had developed a very complicated fracture and they needed to cut the leg. Talandira and the parents were very sad and angry. Why would God give them a child late only to make him lame?

After a few years, a war broke out with a neighbouring village. It was required that all young men should go to the war. Talandira could not go because the had one leg. All the young men in the village went to the war. Unfortunately, the war did not go well. All the young men did not return. They were all killed, including all the sons of the chief. The chief was so heart-broken that he died after a few days. Talandira was the only man who could become the next chief and so he did.

Challenges to the practice of Organizational Learning

In addition to what is said above, there are two main issues that hold back organizational learning and need to be dealt with. These are: fear and impatience.

Fear

> Tatha was an isolated village surrounded by a thick bush. The other villages were far away from it. People usually passed through Tatha to get from one village to another. Because the other villages were so far, the people usually asked for permission to spend a night in the village so that they could continue their journey the next day.
>
> After many years, a problem developed. The travelers who asked to spend the night in the morning would all be dead in the morning. Nobody knew what caused the death. The villagers decided to let no traveler sleep in village any more.
>
> One day, a man arrived in the village. He was very tired and feeling sickly. He persisted that he would sleep and proceed the next day. All efforts to discourage him not to sleep failed. So they let him sleep in the house where all the previous travelers had slept.
>
> At mid-night, he heard some guttural noise. He woke up. What he saw was a strange spectacle. He saw a Monster and a very beautiful young lady standing at the back of the bed he was sleeping on.
>
> "Who is more beautiful, this young lady or myself?" the Monster asked the man.
>
> The man was so frightened – if I say that it is the young lady who is more beautiful, the Monster will kill me – the man thought. He kept his silence.
>
> "Who is more beautiful – this lady or me? The Monster asked again.
>
> "The young lady", the man said and closed his eyes await his fate.
>
> The Monster kept quiet for some time, and then he said:
>
> "All your friends who were passing through this village and spending a night in this house, I killed them. I killed them because they were telling me a lie. They lied to me that I am more beautiful than this beautiful young lady. They were more afraid of me than they were truthful. I am very happy with you. You have told the truth. I wish you all the best for you trip tomorrow. Good night."
>
> With these words the Monster and the beautiful girl disappeared. The man was sweating with both fear and excitement that he was still alive. When he woke up in the morning, the villagers were expecting to find him dead. They were surprised to see him walk out of the house alive.
>
> He explained to the villagers what had happened in the night and why he had survived. "We must tell the truth no matter how fearful we are," he explained to the villagers as he left the village to continue his journey.

Developing organizational effectiveness takes time. The process requires people to be awake and patient.

If you are patient enough, you can see the eyes of a snail

A family organized a party on a weekend and invited some friends to attend. The party started at the lunch hour and went on till the evening.

At around six in the evening, they realized that some of the chicken they had kept for barbecue were missing. They immediately knew the family dog had eaten it. They were so angry. A little drunk, the people caught the dog and tied it to a tree so that they could think of ways to punish it.

They decided to dig a hole and bury the dog alive. They dug a deep hole. They untied the dog from the tree and threw it into the hole. Then, they began to throw soil into the hole in order to bury the dog.

Because it was dark and the people were a little drunk, they could not see properly what was happening in the hole. Whenever they threw in the soil, the dog would shake it off. It kept doing this until the people were almost done in covering the hole. The dog kept quiet until the people finished.

When the people woke up in the morning, they found the dog alive and well moving around the house.

The dog was faced with a death situation, but it survived because of patience.

> It's not that we start out patient. We don't persevere because we are patient people. We become patient because we have to. There is no choice – the work is endless. Every day we have to make a choice. Will we give up, or will we keep on going? When after day we are willing to keep going we discover, quite to our amazement, that we have become patient. And then we just continue on. Day after day. (Wheatley, 2010: 141)

I remember a Margaret Wheatley session I attended in Johannesburg in 2011. Meg had come to South Africa with a group of American and European women to talk about leadership in an African context. I had made an appointment with Meg during that trip. She then asked me to join the women on that day and talk to them about women's leadership during the first session in the morning.

As I sat waiting to be introduced to talk, the session started with the review of the previous day which I had not attended. This was supposed to take 10 minutes. In the process of the review, an issue came up. Two women got very angry because they had perceived their identity was being attacked. These two women talked and talked for close to an hour verbally attacking everyone in the house, particularly Meg.

I was afraid; I didn't know what was going to happen. My talk was apparently forgotten.

When the two women finally stopped talking, Meg calmly said:

"Thank you very much. Any comments from any one on what the two colleagues have expressed?" A few women made more sobered comments.

Then Meg said, "What can we do to address the issue the colleagues have raised?"

There were a few more comments. The issue was resolved in no time and we took a break.

I was so surprised I walked to Meg and asked her – "how do you manage to keep your cool in such situations?"

"Those two women are good. They are not afraid of me or the other women. My responsibility to such people is to be patient in helping them transform their negative energy to positive energy", she said.

Conclusion

Effective organizations will exercise more power and influence. These organizations will be: more interdependent and participative, more humane, less hierarchical and competitive, freer of old discriminations, more networked and nimble and able to acknowledge the diverse strengths and real needs of their members, less tied to old dogmas and more able to learn from experience (CDRA, 2009). These organizations will be based on Ubuntu. Organization Paremiology will be the framework upon which the new development and business in Africa and the world will be based.

EPILOGUE

The Principles and Practice of Organization Paremiology

Introducing Organization Paremiology: An Authentic African Contribution to Global Organizational Effectiveness

During the time I spent working as a consultant on organization development (OD) in Ghana, Malawi, Uganda, Senegal, South Africa, Zimbabwe and Mozambique, I realised an inherent need to have an approach that is relevant to the African context, and one that could make an African contribution to the world of organization development in organizations. This would increase the relevance and legitimacy of current organizational improvement efforts, thereby increasing the sustainability of the efforts.

Based on the foregoing, I thought of the African village as a prototype organization. I asked myself, how was the African community managed? In those times, how were teams built? How was conflict resolved or managed? How was leadership developed? And how was strategic thinking done?

Local communities had specific methods of developing the foregoing. And these methods had been developed over time. I also noted that principles of organization are universal, and that only the practices are different. What happened with the coming of colonialists was that they undermined the local practices, thereby making the locals lose confidence in themselves.

This led to dichotomy or a disconnect whereby the African is divided into two. At work, we have an international identity while at home we have an African identity. This creates a conflict of identity, especially with the African identity suffering. My role was therefore to bring in the African contribution to modern organization development.

In this reflection, I discovered that in the African local community, a key tool for development was wisdom and this wisdom was contained in folktales and proverbs. Proverbs and folktales were the medium by which development was carried out and passed on from generation to generation over a long period of time.

I discovered that just as we use African identity in our personal issues like weddings and funerals, we can use this in our organizational life as well. In organizations, for instance, we use African proverbs to help us in team building, conflict management, strategic development and leadership development. This linking of the indigenous and modern is the essence of this discovery.

The Development Process of Organization Paremiology

1 - How it started

In 1999, I was employed as a trainee OD practitioner by Concern Universal, a British NGO. We were trained for two years in the field of Organizational Development. Our training involved class work, field work and sign posting with organizations doing organizational development in southern Africa.

After the training, we were allowed to start practice. When we started practice, we had challenges: one of the biggest challenges was language. It was difficult to properly translate some organizational development words like strategy and policy into local languages, so that we could communicate properly with local clients. This made me to think about alternatives. Then, I came up with the idea of proverbs and folktales, I discovered that in communities, proverbs or folk tales were used to communicate the issues we were trying to bring about to the communities.

2- How it was developed

In 2002, while on an assignment with COWASH in Phalombe, we lodged in Mulanje. One evening, we went into PTC shop to buy refreshments. While in the shop, we found a BBC focus on Africa magazine and we bought it. In the magazine they were advertising a new book by the BBC on the wisdom of Africa. That evening during our reflection time, I was able to link the wisdom of Africa and the organizational development experience we were having in the villages. By mixing the two, I was able to write the first article, called on 'Using African proverbs in organisational capacity development'. Building on this foundation and the acceptance that the article got, I have authored and published 10 books in which we are using African proverbs as a tool for organizational development.

This is a whole new field of helping organizations to improve their performance based on the wisdom in African proverbs and folktales. The study of African proverbs and folktales is called Paremiology. Since we are talking about applying this wisdom in organizations, I therefore coined the term **Organization Paremiology** for which we are seeking a patent.

3- How it is applied in the organizations

Proverbs identify and dignify a culture. They express the collective wisdom of people, reflecting their thinking, value and behaviour. Using proverbs to communicate and understand organizational issues is a very powerful tool in the quest for a genuine African identity.

In indigenous Africa, proverbs are used to unlock immobility, clarify vision and unify different perspectives. Proverbs add humour and defuse tension on otherwise very sensitive issues. Every African society has used proverbs for centuries to ease uncomfortable situations, confront issues and build institutions and relationships. They can be understood where literacy is low and yet appreciated by even the most educated.

Proverbs are metaphors and can explain complex issues in simple statements. A proverb like A ***stewed liver may look smooth and easy to swallow, but it can choke one to death*** may be a powerful statement in encouraging people to change their sexual behaviour in the fight against HIV and AIDS – i.e. by urging them not to be deceived by how somebody looks and assume that they cannot pass on the virus. Proverbs like ***When one begs for water, it does not quench thirst*** and ***if you borrow a man's legs, you will go where he directs you*** encourage people to be self-reliant and they can explain with more force the concept of sustainability than other conventional methods. A proverb like ***If a mouse is laughing at a cat, it means that it is near a hole*** can be used to discuss strategy when provoked by a seemingly weaker opponent.

Proverbs are like seeds. They only come alive when they are 'sown'. They are simple statements until they get applied to real life situations, bringing them to life and expanding their meaning.

By being metaphorical, proverbs create mental pictures. This is a great tool for motivating people to action.

The Structure and Method of Delivery

Organization Paremiology is delivered through lectures, case studies and general facilitating processes. It is also delivered through written material like books and papers.

We have used African proverbs in Organization Assessment processes, strategic planning, team building, leadership development, board development and self-development interventions. We have also used African proverbs in working with a range of organizations including community based organisations (CBOs), professional NGOs or non-profit organizations, churches and government departments. From these experiences, we have learned a number of lessons.

In the proverbs based self-assessment tools, the proverbs act as a 'communication aid or amplifier'. The participants discuss their understanding of the proverbs. They then apply this understanding when answering a question and determining the assessment rate and its explanation. We have also learned that it is often necessary to use an external facilitator to moderate the discussion and the self-assessment process.

It is necessary to use the most fitting proverbs for the intervention or situation at hand. Using 'loose' proverbs without a clear link to the intervention or the situation may have the effect of confusing the people and disrupting the process. The practitioner must always ask himself or herself the question, what is the most effective proverb that I can use in this situation? In a roles and responsibilities clarification intervention, for example, proverbs like *If the sun says it is more powerful than the moon, let it come and shine at night* and *The cat in his house has the teeth of a lion* may be very appropriate. In communicating the importance of learning from practice, a proverb like *A person is taller than any mountain they have climbed* would be appropriate.

In training workshops, it is important to use only a few proverbs to maximise their impact. Too many proverbs may lead to loss of interest in the proverbs. This also applies to carrying out assessments using the proverbs based tools. In a three-day team-building workshop, for example, we use about three proverbs in one session at the beginning of the workshop to bring to the surface issues and insights for discussion. In the proverbs based assessment tool this may mean that not all categories may need the proverbs – only those for which proverbs will add significant value. In other words, proverbs are more useful where a direct question may not bring out all the insights because people do not completely understand the question or the issue.

It is important to use reflective questions in order to bring out the insights from proverbs. Since proverbs may mean different things to different people at different times and in different contexts, the questions must be properly phrased and focused to enable them to solicit only these insights related to the issue at hand. In self-development sessions, for example, we use a question like: What insights on self-development can we learn from the proverb ***A changed place cannot transform an individual, but a transformed individual can change a place?*** When we used this question and proverb with a rural CBO, a chief explained his total agreement with the proverb by telling the group the story of an individual in his village who migrated to a neighbouring country, hoping to be 'transformed' by its better economy, and somebody else, a very productive individual, who had come to reside in his village and had become very worthy within a short time. The person who migrated to the other country came back frustrated and poorer after a few years, owing to the fact that the 'transformed nation' had failed to transform him.

Proverbs can also be reflective case studies. To do this more effectively, it is important to know and use the story upon which the proverbs are based. Using a story is especially useful on complicated issues, which are difficult to communicate. For example, it is extremely difficult to teach and communicate organizational identity issues, but using 'proverb case studies' easily transcends such a barrier. In 'identity interventions', for example, we have used the story behind the proverb ***An eaglet that does know it is an eagle, may live like a chicken.*** The story goes like this…

A farmer picked an egg from an eagle's nest. He placed it among the eggs a chicken was sitting on. When the eggs hatched, there was an eaglet from the eagle's egg among the chicks. The eaglet and the chicks grew and moved around together. Because of its socialisation, the eaglet took the personality of a chick and was growing into a chicken until one day an eagle that was flying over the chicken and the chicks noticed the eaglet.

The eagle descended and hovered over the chicken and the chicks, calling out to the eaglet. The chicken and the chicks became restless and afraid and were running for cover. The eaglet too became restless and afraid and was running for cover. In the process, however, the eaglet looked up and was immediately struck by the resemblance with the eagle. For the first time, the eaglet saw that it was different from the chicken and chicks. Instead of causing more fear, the calls of the eagle started to create a strong attraction on the eaglet. The eaglet felt like getting closer to the eagle. That moment the eaglet knew that it did not belong to the chickens anymore. The eaglet had never flown before. It tried to jump and the moment this happened, it flew away with mother eagle.

Discussion questions:

1. What does the story of the eaglet teach us as an organization?
2. How similar or different are we to the eaglet?
3. What are we going to do in order to improve?

Finally, proverbs must be used naturally and flexibly, not mechanically. The proverbs may actually become a hindrance to the process. The power of proverbs, when used properly, is their 'invisibility' as they serve to facilitate the process rather than draw attention to themselves. This means the proverbs must be used only when their use will add value to the process. Development practitioners must not get too excited with the use of proverbs to the extent of 'using crutches when they can walk on their own feet'.

Resources

The resources required for delivery are produced by Dr Malunga, who has written ten other books on the subject. The

10 books Dr Malunga has authored on this subject are the only resources in the world on Organization Paremiology.

The books are listed below: (Please add the full publication details for each of the books, including year of publication, etc).

1. Understanding Organisational Sustainability through African proverbs
   By Dr Chiku Malunga
   Published by Practical Action Publishers, United Kingdom
2. Making Strategic Plans work: Insights from African Indigenous Wisdom
   By Dr Chiku Malunga
   Published by Adonis and Abbey
   United Kingdom
3. Understanding Organizational Leadership Through Ubuntu
   By Dr Chiku Malunga
   Published by Adonis and Abbey
   United Kingdom
4. Power and Influence: Self-development Lessons from African Proverbs and folktales
   By Dr Chiku Malunga
   Published by University Press of America
5. Cultivating Personal and Organizational Effectiveness: Spiritual Insights from African Proverbs
   By Chiku Malunga
   Published by University Press of America
6. Organizational Wisdom in 100 African Proverbs: An introduction to Organization Paremiology
   By Dr Chiku Malunga
   Published by Adonis and Abbey
7. Endogenous Development
   By Dr Chiku Malunga
   Co-edited with Prof Susan Holcombe
   Published by Routledge Publishers, USA

8. NGO management
   By Dr Chiku Malunga Co-edited with Prof Alan Fowler
   Published by Earthscan Publishers, United Kingdom
9. Animal Farm Prophecy Fulfilled in Africa: A Call to Values
   and Systems Revolution
   By Dr Chiku Malunga
   Published by University Press of America.

Selected References

Aiken, M. and Brittan, B. 1997. The Learning Organization and the Voluntary Sector in Janice et al. The Learning Organization in the Public Services

Andersen, R. 2008. The Executive Calling. Florida. Creation House

Ayres, J. 2015. What does OD do in the World, What is the reason for its Expansion? News, May 2015

Belaymah. M 2013. Education Theory, Practice. Rote Vs Meaningful Learning http:llcommons.wikimedia.org/wiki/ 17b October

Canfield, J. 2007. How to Get from Where You are to Where You want to be: The 25 Principles of Success, Harper-Element: London

CDRA, 2009.2009. Barefoot to Working with Organizations and Social Change, CDRA, Cape Town, South Africa

Coelho, P. 2003. Warrior of the Light. Happer, New York.

Collins J. 2001. Good to Great. Harper Business London

Collins. J and Hansen. M 2011. Great by Choice. Harper Business London

Conger, J. 1998: The Charismatic Leader: Behind the Mystique of Exceptional Leadership. Jossey-Bass Publishers, San Francisco

Covey. S. 2004. The 8th Habit: From Effectiveness to Greatness. Simon Schuter. London

Drucker, P. 1997. Adventures of a Bysatander, John Wiley and Sons, London

Edwards, M. 1996. Becoming a Learning Organization – Unpublished paper, Aga Khan Foundation of Canada.

Fowler, A 1997. Striking a Balance. Earthscan: London

Harrington and Mackin, 2013: Survival of the Hive: 7 Leadership Lessons from the Beehive, AuthorHouse, UK

King, C, Washington, J. and Ammeh, S. 2008. A Testament of Hope: Words and Speeches of Martin Luther King and Barrack Obama, Self Improvement Publishing, Benin City, Nigeria

King, M. 1969. Strength to Love, London, Fontana Books

Malunga, 2009. Understanding Organizational Sustainability through Ubuntu, Adonis &Abbey, London

Malunga, 2010. Oblivion or Utopia: The Prospects for Africa, University Press of America, Lanham Maryland

Malunga, 2014; Organizational Wisdom in 100 African Proverbs, London, Adonis and Abbey Publishers

Malunga. C, 2000: The Beehive Model for Team Building, Footsteps Magazine no 43200

Malunga. C, 2009: Understanding Organizational Leadership through Ubuntu, Adonis & Abbey, London, UK

Munroe, M. 2005. The Spirit of Leadership. Whitaker House. New Kensington

Nee. W. 1965. Release of the Spirit. New Wine Press. London

Rische, J. And Van Gorden, 2008. The Kingdom of the Occult

Sanders, J. 1994. Spiritual Leadership, Chicago. Moody Press

Schein, D. 2010. Organizational Culture and Leadership, London, Jossey – Bass

Ubels, Acquaye – Badoo; and Fowler, 2010: Capacity Development in Practice, London, Francis and Taylor

Weisz. P, 1967: The Science of Biology, McGraw Hill Book Company. New York

Wheatley, M.2010. Perseverance. Berkana Publication. Provo Utah

Wigglesworth, S. 2000. Greater Works: Experiencing God's Power, Whitaker House, New Kensington

www.Honey.com/kids

Index